TOWARD A MORE PERFECT UNION: SIX ESSAYS ON THE ★ ★ ★ CONSTITUTION ★ ★ ★

TOWARD A MORE PERFECT UNION: SIX ESSAYS ON THE ★ ★ ★ CONSTITUTION ★ ★ ★

EDITED BY

Neil L. York

BRIGHAM YOUNG UNIVERSITY

Library of Congress Cataloging-in-Publication Data

Toward a more perfect union: six essays on the Constitution
edited by Neil L. York
188 pages
Bibliography: p. 175
Includes index
1. United States—Constitutional history.
I. York, Neil L., 1951–
KF4541.A2T69   1988   342.73′029—dc19   [347.30229]   88-14507
                                                                                CIP

ISBN 0-88706-925-8
ISBN 0-88706-926-6 (pbk.)

Brigham Young University, Provo, Utah 84602
"1787 and 1776: Patrick Henry, James Madison, the Constitution,
and the Revolution," © 1988 by Lance Banning
"States, Sections, and the National Interest," © 1988 by Peter
S. Onuf
© 1988 by Brigham Young University. All rights reserved
Printed in the United States of America

Distributed by State University of New York Press,
State University Plaza, Albany, New York 12446-0001

Contents

Editor's Note:

As there are numerous references to, and quotations of, the *Federalist* throughout this volume, for ease of location all citations are to Clinton Rossiter, ed., *The Federalist Papers: Alexander Hamilton, James Madison, John Jay* (New York: New American Library, 1961). Such references and quotations are cited in the notes with *Federalist,* followed by the number of the particular paper, followed by a colon and the page number(s) where the reference or quotation can be found in the New American Library edition. For example, quotation of the first line of *Federalist* No. 10 would be cited as *Federalist* 10:77. In a few instances, page numbers (inside parentheses) immediately follow quotations in the text and notes.

Introduction

In his 1987 presidential address to the Organization of American Historians, Leon Litwack warned against being swept up in Bicentennial hoopla.[1] For too many, he feared, celebration of the "founding" would provide an excuse for parades and parties rather than a time for introspection and reevaluation; the Constitution, after all, is venerated by most Americans as "holy writ"—a fundamental testament of national ideals.[2] That it has become a source of great pride and is somehow inseparable from an American sense of political self should not be surprising. By attaching such significance to it we are following the lead of Aristotle, who declared that the forming of a constitution is the most important step in organizing a political society. Nevertheless, Aristotle was not always clear in explaining what he meant by constitution. He ambiguously described a constitution as "the arrangement of the inhabitants of a state" as well as "the arrangement of power in a state"; he spoke, confusingly, of a constitution as being synonymous with government and yet greater than government because it was concerned first and foremost with the definition of citizenship.[3]

Americans escaped some of the ambiguities of Aristotle's constitution when writing their own "Constitution"—a document of ink on parchment, a tangible embodiment of Aristotle's more abstract notion. Yet Americans can wander off into their own ambiguities and inconsistencies when interpreting their Constitution, especially when they conflate that Constitution with constitutionalism and the age-old attempt to define rights under law. It should be remembered that the Constitution of 1787 followed a long line of earlier constitutions. Colonial Americans had claimed "constitutional" rights derived from their charters; before 1776 they repeatedly attempted to establish and secure liberties they believed were protected under the unwritten English constitution. State constitution-making during the Revolutionary era and adoption of the Articles of Confederation preserved the connection to that tradition even as Americans struck out on their own. So, too, did the Declaration of Independence by marking (at least symbolically) the emergence of a distinct people committed to the promotion of freedom and rights. The Framers of the Constitution understood this even if many contemporary Americans do not. Indeed, for some Americans of the current generation the Constitution of 1787 has been their only "true" constitution. There was no other before it and nothing could ever take its place.

Present preferences aside, in 1787 there were men of good conscience and wide political experience who objected to the new frame of government that came out of the Philadelphia Convention. They continued to support the Articles of Confederation as the best "constitution" for the nation, and they opposed the "consolidated" government that the Constitution would bring with it. Gone, they argued, would be the federalism they trusted in, destroyed along with the revolutionary principles of 1776. Although they lost the debate and the Articles were cast aside, objections to the Constitution and desires to modify or move beyond it did not end with their defeat.

Christian zealots and statesmen such as Thomas Jefferson fretted over the silence of the Constitution on the subject of religion, but for very different reasons. Jefferson worried because the Constitution did not expressly guarantee complete freedom of religion, where everyone had the right to believe and worship—or disbelieve and shun church; zealots were anxious because the Constitution did not ban atheists or infidels from holding high office. James Madison wanted to prevent the overextension of national power under a constitution that he helped draft. Even so, because he wanted to insure that future generations of virtuous men would be trained to lead the people, as president he echoed George Washington in calling for a university funded and erected by the national government. Madison, then, joined Jefferson and other leaders who were obliged to define and redefine the limits of government as they put the Constitution into practice.

What, for example, came first, state or national citizenship? The Constitution was all but silent on this question, skirting the very issue that Aristotle had contended constitutions were expected to define. During the Philadelphia Convention William Samuel Johnson had observed that the "controversy must be endless whilst Gentlemen differ in the grounds of their arguments," dividing between "those on one side considering the States as districts of people composing one political society" and "those on the other considering them as so many political societies."[4] Civil war four generations later was a bloody reminder of the cost of leaving such questions unanswered. It likewise showed that the Constitution was morally ambiguous because it sanctioned the existence of slavery, reflecting the Founders' choice of "the slaveholders right to property" over "the slaves right to liberty."[5] Reconstruction brought an end to slavery and thereby, through amendment, freed the Constitution from its "covenant with death,"[6] but the full blessings of citizenship were not extended immediately to emancipated slaves—or to Indians or women and others kept on the fringe of public life. Critics of the Constitution conclude that for this and other reasons the Constitution has been, as one put it, a "huge flop."[7]

The past Bicentennial year saw the Iran-Contra hearings, which caused a few—not many, but a few—to ask if the Constitution is working at all. During that same year Archibald Cox completed his book on the Supreme Court and the Constitution. Despite his having been fired as a special prosecutor in the notorious "Saturday Night Massacre" of October 1973, or perhaps because of the way that the larger Watergate crisis was resolved less than a year later, Cox concluded that the Constitution "serves us well."[8] That, by and large, seems to be the opinion of most Americans.

Their general popularity notwithstanding, the Constitution and the men who made it are not easy to explain; historians who have made the attempt often (and quite naturally) disagree over what the Founders intended to do as well as over what they ended up doing. Although the Bicentennial of the Constitution did not (and could not) bring a scholarly consensus, those who study the "founding" reached a wider national audience.

Beginning in 1985 and continuing for the next two years, Brigham Young University sponsored a series of lectures on the Constitution.[9] The participants in the 1987 program delivered addresses drawn from the essays printed here. One additional essay was written later just for this volume, bringing the total to six. All of the authors long pondered the issues before they accepted the Founders' "standing invitation" to review once again the handiwork of the Philadelphia Convention.[10] As students of a bygone era they could do no more; as scholars seeking to improve our understanding they could do no less.

NEIL L. YORK
March 1988

Notes

1. Leon Litwack, "Trouble in Mind: The Bicentennial and the Afro-American Experience," *Journal of American History* 74 (1987): 313–37.

2. James Oliver Robertson, *American Myth, American Reality* (New York: Hill and Wang, 1980), 65–69.

3. Richard McKeon, ed., *The Basic Works of Aristotle* (New York: Random House, 1941), in "Politics," bk. 3, chap. 1, pp. 1176, 1178; bk. 3, chap. 7, p. 1185; bk. 4, chap. 1, p. 1206. "Constitution" is often used as the translation for the Greek *politeia;* the terms are not perfectly interchangeable, just as our modern notions about the relationship of law to society differ from those of the Greeks.

4. As taken from Max Farrand, ed., *The Records of the Federal Convention of 1787,* rev. ed., 4 vols. (New Haven: Yale University Press, 1937), 1:461; Johnson's words as recorded by Madison.

5. Morton White, *Philosophy,* The Federalist, *and the Constitution* (New York: Oxford University Press, 1987), 221–22.

6. William Lloyd Garrison characterized the Constitution as a "covenant with death." See Paul Finkelman, *An Imperfect Union* (Chapel Hill: University of North Carolina Press, 1981); and Finkelman, "Slavery and the Constitutional Convention: Making a Covenant With Death," in Richard Beeman et al., eds., *Beyond Confederation: Origins of the Constitution and American National Identity* (Chapel Hill: University of North Carolina Press, 1987), 188–225.

7. Ferdinand Lundberg, *Cracks in the Constitution* (Secaucus, N.J.: Lyle Stuart, 1980), 42.

8. Archibald Cox, *The Court and the Constitution* (Boston: Houghton Mifflin, 1987), 26.

9. The papers for these programs have been published in Gary C. Bryner and Noel B. Reynolds, eds., *Constitutionalism and Rights* (Provo, Utah: Brigham Young University, 1987); and Gary C. Bryner and Dennis L Thompson, eds., *The Constitution and the Regulation of Society* (Provo, Utah: Brigham Young University, 1988).

10. Philip Kurland and Ralph Lerner, eds., *The Founders' Constitution,* 5 vols. (Chicago: University of Chicago Press, 1987), 1:xiii, noted that the Founders, by their extensive correspondence and record keeping, in effect left a "standing invitation" for later generations to examine what they had done.

The July 1987 issue of *The William and Mary Quarterly* focused on the Constitution and included a "Forum" on Gordon S. Wood's *The Creation of the American Republic, 1776–1787* (Chapel Hill: University of North Carolina Press, 1969). The twelve essayists in this forum, distinguished scholars all, concurred that Wood's study deserves its reputation as a "modern classic"—a "tour de force," as one put it. In a sense Wood had answered his own call, made three years before the book was published, for intellectual history that went beyond the mere explication of ideas, a new approach that dug beneath the surface to expose the underlying political culture. For his efforts he received the Bancroft and John H. Dunning book prizes.

Wood's book was a revised version of his 1964 doctoral dissertation, written under Bernard Bailyn at Harvard University. Born in nearby Concord, Massachusetts, in 1933, Wood did his undergraduate work at Tufts University. He was a postdoctoral fellow at the Institute of Early American History and Culture in Williamsburg, Virginia, and taught at Harvard and the University of Michigan before taking his post as professor of history at Brown University. In 1982–83 he was Pitt Professor of American History at Cambridge University.

It would be impossible for Professor Wood to summarize in a brief essay the six hundred carefully crafted pages of *The Creation of the American Republic*. He has, however, extracted one major theme for discussion here—namely, he contends that the Framers of the Constitution broadened the old idea of popular sovereignty to a new conception of the people and constituent power. They made the people the arbiters of political legitimacy and yet, at the same time, they hoped that government would be led by a virtuous elite. Through all of this they were only partially aware that they had created a "new science of politics."

I

THE POLITICAL
IDEOLOGY OF
THE FOUNDERS

★

Gordon S. Wood

Political ideology—that's not the way we usually describe the thought of the Founders. Political philosophy, political theory, or political ideas perhaps, but not "ideology." The term smacks too much of deception, of superstructure, of rationalization, of a covering of some sort, of ideas being used to mask some deeper-lying social interests.

Yet "political ideology" was the term suggested to me by the editor of these essays, and I think it is an appropriate term for a historian to use. For political thought studied historically is always ideology, always rooted in specific social circumstances. Historians by trade are interested in the particular sources of ideas in particular times and places. They want to know why specific individuals spoke and wrote as they did. But ideas do not have to remain ideology, do not have to remain rooted in specific circumstances of time and place. What particular individuals spoke and wrote can transcend those individuals' intentions, interests, and desires and become part of the public culture, become something larger and grander than its sources. That is certainly what happened with the political ideology of the Founders.

Many of the great constitutional principles celebrated during these Bicentennial occasions—separation of powers, federalism, checks and balances, judicial review, popular sovereignty—were not clearly in the minds of the Framers in the summer of 1787 when they set about the business of forming a new national government. Americans had used several of these terms—such as separation of powers, balanced government, or popular sovereignty—earlier in 1776 when they formed their revolutionary state constitutions; but the terms then did not have the meanings they would later acquire as a consequence of the making of the federal Constitution of 1787. The truth is that many of our most cherished principles of constitutionalism associated with the founding of the national government were created, so to speak, inadvertently. They were the products not of closet philosophizing but of contentious political polemics. The Framers were not ivory-tower academics working out their political theories in the quiet of a study (though some of them, like James Madison, tried to do just that). They were political leaders, with constituencies and interests to protect and promote, and they were caught up in perhaps the greatest crisis of their crisis-filled lives. Thus they were usually compelled to think, as it were, on their feet, in the heat and urgency of debate.

They were not scholars, at least not in any modern sense of the term; they were not demigods; they were not even geniuses; but they were thoughtful, articulate, often well-read men who usually thought of their audience as men like themselves, which is the major reason the learned quality of their thinking has not generally been duplicated by later American political leaders. Democracy and equality are good things, but they did not come cheap. One of the prices we Americans have had to pay for them was a change in the character of our political rhetoric from that high level common to the Revolutionary era.

The changes were occurring even as the Framers debated the Constitution. The members of the Philadelphia Convention went to extraordinary lengths to keep their proceedings secret in order to protect the delegates' freedom of expression. The result was a degree of candor and boldness by the delegates in discussing sensitive issues like aristocracy and popular power that is notably missing from the debates in the various state ratifying conventions held several months later. Since the ratifying conventions were open to the press, the difference in tone and character of the respective debates reveals just what a broader, more democratic public could mean for the intellectual life of American politics.

Broadening and deepening the audience for political rhetoric may have meant a certain loss of candor and perhaps in time a lessening of intellectual quality, but at the moment in 1787–88 it was the cause of the Founders' creativity and originality. Precisely because the Framers had to explain and justify the new Constitution to a broader and more democratic public than had ever existed in America before, they were forced to put their thoughts in forms palatable to this new public. They had to reconcile their new Constitution with democracy—to find, as James Madison put it, "a republican remedy for the diseases most incident to republican government."[1] In the end this democratic pressure, this need to persuade a growing and skeptical public of the popular character of the new government, made all the difference. It was the source of the Founders' intellectual achievement.

Reconciling the new Constitution with popular principles was not easy. There is little doubt that on its face the Constitution violated much of the conventional popular thinking of late eighteenth-century America. It was a very radical proposal, more radical than we today can properly appreciate. We today are too used to a strong national government to understand how unexpected, how remarkable in 1787 the Constitution was. In place of the Articles of Confederation, a league or alliance of independent states, it created a strong unitary national government that operated directly on individuals. No one in 1776 had predicted or had wanted such a strong government. Such national power was then beyond anyone's wildest dreams. The colonists in the British empire had experienced enough abuses from far-removed governmental power to make them deeply fearful of creating another distant and powerful government. And had not the best minds of the eighteenth century, including Montesquieu, repeatedly told them that a large continental-size republic was a theoretical impossibility?

Something momentous happened in the decade following 1776 to change American thinking so dramatically. We are apt to think, as many historians have, that it was the accumulated deficiencies of the Articles of Confederation that lay behind the move for a new national Constitution. It is true that there were national problems of taxation, of commerce, of credit, of foreign policy that made many leaders increasingly disgusted with what they called the "imbecility" of the Confederation. By 1787 nearly everyone, even those who would later oppose the Constitution, expected something to be done to strengthen the Articles of Confederation. "It is on all hands acknowledged," declared a Massachusetts opponent of the Constitution, "that the federal government is not adequate to the purpose of the Union."[2] Many Americans shared a deeply felt vision of the United States as a single nation and wanted a firmer union. But many of them also knew that the principal weaknesses of the Confederation and the strengthening of union could be solved without totally scrapping the Articles of Confederation and creating a radically powerful national government, the like of which had not been even conceived of ten years earlier.

The widespread concern both for the inadequacies of the Confederation and the nationhood of the United States was important: it gave the Framers of the Constitution their initial opportunity and advantage. It accounts for the remarkably casual acceptance of the May 1787 meeting in Philadelphia by many later opponents of the Constitution, and in the end it may account for the eventual reluctant acceptance of the Constitution by many of these same opponents. But the weaknesses of the Confederation and the dream of nationhood, however keenly felt, cannot ultimately explain the nature of the Constitution proposed by the Philadelphia Convention, not to mention the extraordinary Virginia Plan which was the Convention's working model.

The fact of the matter is that the Convention went far beyond what most people expected, went far beyond the charge given it by the Confederation Congress in February 1787—to meet "for the sole and express purpose of revising the Articles of Confederation."[3] Instead the Convention ignored the Articles of Confederation and created in its place a totally different and unexpectedly powerful national government.

It did so because the men there were worried about more than just the problems of the Confederation: they were worried about the problems of the states as well. Indeed, it was the oppressive behavior of the state legislatures that was uppermost in the minds of most of the Framers. The state legislatures were the most democratic and most representative lawmaking bodies in the world. They were the true testing ground of the Americans' revolutionary experiment in popular government. And therefore failure in these democratic state legislatures was no simple practical matter; it struck at the heart of what the Revolution was

about. For abuses by popularly elected legislatures, said James
Madison, brought "into question the fundamental principle of
republican government, that the majority who rule in such governments are the safest guardians both of public good and private
rights."[4]

In 1776 the Revolutionaries had placed great confidence in the
ability of the state legislatures to promote the public good and
protect the people's liberties. After all, had not the various colonial legislatures been the great bulwarks of defense against the
power of the royal governors? In their revolutionary state constitutions written in 1776–77 Americans had increased the size of
their state legislatures, made them more equally representative of
the people than the colonial assemblies had been, and granted
enormous power to them. But in the years after 1776 these state
legislatures did not live up to the initial expectations of many of
America's leaders. The Revolution unleashed acquisitive and factional economic interests that no one had quite realized existed in
American society; and in the decade after Independence these
partial factional interests demanded and got protection and satisfaction from state legislatures that were now elected annually (an
innovation for most) by the broadest electorates in the world.
Everywhere in the states electioneering and the open competition
for office increased, as new petty, uneducated entrepreneurs like
Abraham Yates, a part-time lawyer and shoemaker of Albany,
and William Findley, a Scots-Irish ex-weaver of western Pennsylvania, used popular electoral appeals to vault into political leadership in the state legislatures.

No one saw more clearly what was happening than did James
Madison. In the winter of 1786–87 he put his ideas together in a
working paper that he called "vices of the political system of the
United States." It formed the basis of many of his ideas expressed
during the debate over the Constitution. In this paper he concentrated on the deficiencies of the state legislatures. These legislatures were swallowing up the powers of the other branches of the
state governments and were passing multitudes of special-interest
legislation—stay laws, paper money bills, and other debtor relief
laws—in violation of the rights of creditors and other minorities.
There were more laws passed than people could keep up with, in
fact, said Madison, more laws in the decade since independence
than in the previous century of colonial history.

Madison's disgust with the oppressive vagaries of state lawmaking did not come from reading all those bundles of books that Jefferson was sending him from Paris. He learned about the vices of state legislative politics firsthand—as a member of the Virginia Assembly between 1784 and 1787.

Madison had some notable legislative achievements during these years, particularly Jefferson's bill for religious freedom. But generally his experience as a legislator was not a happy one. It was not what he had expected from republicanism and popular government. Really for the first time he found out what democracy in America might mean. Many of his fellow legislators were not like him or Jefferson. They had never been to William and Mary, let alone Princeton. They were narrow-minded and parochial and were bent on serving some "particular interest." They had little comprehension of the collective good—not even that of Virginia, never mind that of the United States. They did not even seem to understand the legislative process. They postponed taxes, subverted debts owed to the subjects of Great Britain, and passed, defeated, and repassed bills in the most haphazard manner. Madison found himself having to make legislative deals and trade-offs, agreeing to bad laws for fear of getting worse ones, or giving up good bills "rather than pay such a price" as his opponents wanted. Many of the legislators pandered to the public, especially to its "itch for paper money," and were always trying to appear popular. This appealing to the people as the ultimate arbiter had none of the beneficial effects good republicans had expected. A bill having to do with court reform was, for example, "to be printed for consideration of the public"; but "instead of calling for the sanction of the wise and virtuous," this appeal to the people, Madison feared, would only "be a signal to interested men to redouble their efforts to get into the Legislature." Democracy was no solution to the problem; democracy was the problem.[5]

What the Virginia legislature was doing in the 1780s does not strike us today as all that unusual or alarming, and we can scarcely muster much sympathy for Madison's complaints. He only described what we now take for granted and what we have become very used to—good old popular American politics with all its horsetrading and pork barreling. We are not surprised or upset when representatives say they have to look after their constituents' interests. We are used to our politicians running scared and being worried about their particular districts. That is what American democratic politics is about.

However disillusioned Madison was with this democratic politics—this incessant scrambling for interests, this continual pandering to voters—he knew now that it was an ineradicable part of American social reality. People had interests: that is all there was to it. Because they wanted to protect their interests, they divided into political factions. The causes of faction were, quite simply, "sown in the nature of man."[6] It was utopian to expect most people to put aside these interests for the sake of some nebulous public good. And it would be a denial of liberty to try to eliminate them. Yet Madison hoped that the new federal Constitution would somehow be able to solve this problem of American democratic politics and transcend the problem of self-interested and tyrannical majorities. "It may be asked," he said, "how private rights will be more secure under the guardianship of the General Government than under the state governments, since they are both founded on the republican principle which refers the ultimate decision to the will of the majority."[7] What, in other words, was really different about the new national government from the state governments that would keep it from succumbing to the same popular pressures from special-interest majorities as were besetting the state governments in the 1780s?

What would be different, Madison and the other Federalists hoped, would be the character of the persons holding office in the new national government. What they wanted in office were more men who possessed "the most attractive merit and the most diffusive and established characters"; gentlemen who were well known, liberally educated, cosmopolitan, and virtuous; gentlemen who were capable of "disinterested" judgment.[8]

"Disinterested" was a common term men like Madison invoked. They meant by it not what today we often mean—uninterested or unconcerned—but rather impartial and unbiased by personal advantage. A "disinterested" person was not someone who had no interests or did not care about them but rather someone who did not allow his concern for his private interests to affect his judgment. Ideally a public official was to be a "disinterested and dispassionate umpire," someone who was most capable of transcending his own private interests and those of others and of deciding what was in the public interest of the whole community.[9]

Who were most likely to be such disinterested and dispassionate umpires, men capable of standing above the various contending interests of the society? The Federalists thought that such leaders were most apt to come from the ranks of gentlemen. "Gentleman" was a term of great significance for the eighteenth century, one that we today have almost totally lost. Then it was ideally confined to a tiny proportion of the society, to men with sufficient independence, wealth, and leisure that they did not have to work or exert themselves in the mean and sordid business of making money in the marketplace. This vision of a leisured aristocracy being the best source of political leadership went back to classical antiquity, to Aristotle and Cicero. In the eighteenth-century English-speaking world the ideal seemed best embodied in the English landed gentry, who lived off rents from their tenants. To Adam Smith these rents were what gave the English landed aristocracy its unique qualifications to be disinterested public leaders. Their income from rents, said Smith, "costs them neither labour nor care, but comes to them as it were, of its own accord, and independent of any plan or project of their own." Therefore these landed gentry, "being attached to no particular occupation themselves, have leisure and inclination to examine the occupations of other people." They were best equipped to be disinterested and dispassionate umpires, which may help explain why the English landed aristocracy maintained its political dominance in Great Britain as long as it did. [10]

In America there was no ready equivalent of this English landed aristocracy. Wealthy southern slaveholding gentry obviously came closest to this English ideal, but their income scarcely came without exertion and their slaves were hardly comparable to English tenants. The southern planters, despite their strenuous efforts to hide the fact, were deeply involved in the vicissitudes and dependencies of the international marketing of staple crops. In the north, leisured, independent gentry were even harder to find. Merchants, no matter how wealthy, were tainted by their participation in trade. Therefore, those merchants who wanted to become public leaders usually had to abandon their businesses and ennoble themselves in order to gain full acceptance as public leaders. John Hancock, George Clymer, Henry Laurens, Elbridge Gerry, and eventually even Robert Morris all shed their merchant businesses during the Revolution in hopes of convincing people of their capacity for disinterestedness.

Mechanics or artisans who worked with their hands were disqualified for high public office by definition; they were not even gentlemen. The big question was whether or not members of the professions, such as lawyers, were capable of disinterested service. Alexander Hamilton argued strongly in *The Federalist* that, unlike merchants, mechanics, or farmers, "the learned professions . . . truly form no distinct interest in society"; thus they "will feel a neutrality to the rivalships between the different branches of industry" and will be most likely to be "an impartial arbiter" between the diverse interests of a marketplace society.[11] Others, however, were not so sure; and the argument over the potential disinterestedness of the professions continued well into the nineteenth century, and in a different form even into our own time.

However unsentimental and realistic Madison was about the interested nature of man and the prevalence of clashing interests in society, he still clung to the ancient classical ideal of disinterested leadership. He still hoped against hope that in the new federal system it might be possible amid all the competing private and factional interests for a few enlightened men of education and liberal sentiments to gain office and act in a disinterested manner.

How was this to be done? By elevating and enlarging the arena of politics. Raising important governmental decision making to the national level would expand the electorate for each official and at the same time would reduce the number of those elected. This elevated government and expanded electorate would then act as a kind of filter, refining the kind of men who would become national leaders. In a larger arena with a smaller number of representatives, only the most notable, the most educated, the most disinterested were likely to gain political office. If the people of North Carolina, for example, could select only five men to the federal Congress in contrast to the 232 they elected to their state assembly, they were more apt in the case of the few national representatives to ignore obscure ordinary men with "factious tempers" and "local prejudices" and elect those gentry with "the most attractive merit and the most diffusive and established characters."[12] We have only to compare the small number of sixty-five representatives who sat in the first national Congress with the thousand or more representatives in the state legislatures in order to understand what this narrowing and refining process of the Federalists might mean. As one Georgia Federalist put it, in the new national government "none will be distinguished with places of trust but those who possess superior talents and accomplishments."[13] The Federalists' political ideology rested on a particular insight into the sociology of American politics.

No wonder, then, that the opponents of the Constitution—the Antifederalists—charged that the new national government was rushing Americans into aristocracy. They saw at once the social implications of this elevated federal government where presumably only "high-toned" and "great men" would hold office. This Constitution, they said, was designed to "raise the fortunes and respectability of the well-born few, and oppress the plebians." The Antifederalists opposed the new government for precisely the same social reasons that the Federalists favored it.[14]

Yet the Federalists knew that in the growing egalitarian atmosphere of America they could no longer openly defend aristocracy, even a natural aristocracy. They anticipated the Antifederalists' objections. "When this plan goes forth," John Dickinson warned the Philadelphia Convention, "it will be attacked by popular leaders, aristocracy will be the watchword; the Shibboleth among its adversaries." Precisely because the Antifederalists, as Alexander Hamilton observed in the New York ratifying convention, did talk "so often of an aristocracy," the Federalists were continually compelled to play down or disguise the social expectations and implications of the Constitution.[15] They felt the need to say over and over how popular and democratic the new system was. Much of *The Federalist,* for example, was devoted to demonstrating just how "strictly republican" the Constitution was. Of the six "particulars" that "Publius," in *Federalist* No. 1, said he intended to discuss, the fourth, "The conformity of the proposed Constitution to the true principles of republican government," took up forty-eight of the eighty-five essays.[16]

In the various state ratifying conventions the Federalists went out of their way to stress their commitment to popular government. "The supporters of the Constitution," declared John Marshall in the Virginia Convention, "claim the title of being firm friends of the liberty and the rights of mankind." The Federalists, he said, were the real protectors of the people; they "idolize democracy." Far from being supporters of aristocracy, the Federalists admired the Constitution precisely because they "think it a well-regulated democracy."[17]

Under the polemical pressure placed on them by the opponents of the Constitution, the Federalists were compelled to think freshly and to create something more than they intended. Their political thinking soon came to transcend its purposes. By being forced to debate and answer the objections of the Antifederalists, the Federalists were led into developing arguments and positions that they otherwise might not have made. The result was the most creative and significant moment of theorizing about politics in our nation's history. Simply because they forced this debate and the creative achievements that followed from it, the Antifederalists deserve to be numbered among the Founders.

To the Antifederalists the Constitution created a republic of continental size that violated the principles of the best political thinking of the day. Montesquieu among others had warned that a republic, precisely because it rested on the consent of the people, had to be small in size and homogeneous in character. If it were too big, composed of too many different groups and interests, it would be torn apart by factionalism and clashes among these opposing interests. It was impossible for a single government to comprehend both Georgia and Massachusetts. The very idea of a single republic "on an average one thousand miles in length, and eight hundred in breadth, and containing six million of white inhabitants all reduced to the same standard of morals, of habits, and of laws, is," said the Antifederalists, "in itself an absurdity, and contrary to the whole experience of mankind."[18]

These were the old-fashioned theories of 1776, wrote Madison with a decade's experience behind him. Americans, he said, used to think that the people composing a republic "enjoy not only an equality of political rights, but that they have all precisely the same interests and the same feelings in every respect." Such a republic had to be small in size in order to maintain this similarity of feelings and interests. It was assumed in such a small republic that "the interest of the majority would be that of the minority also; the decisions could only turn on mere opinion concerning the good of the whole of which the major voice would be the safest criterion; and within a small sphere this voice could be most easily collected and the public affairs most accurately managed." Now, however, to Madison and other disillusioned Federalists, this assumption about republicanism seemed "altogether fictitious." No society, no matter how small, "ever did or can consist of so homogeneous a mass of citizens." All "civilized societies" were made up of "various and unavoidable" distinctions: rich and poor, creditors and debtors, farmers and manufacturers, merchants and bankers, and so on.[19]

In a small republic it was sometimes possible for one of these competing interests or factions to gain majority control of a legislature and become oppressive. This problem of tyrannical majority factions was the cause of the crisis of republicanism in the 1780s. "To secure the public good and private rights against the danger of such a faction, and at the same time to preserve the spirit and the form of popular government," wrote Madison, was "the great object to which our inquiries are directed."[20]

Madison and other Federalists solved the problem by turning the conventional assumptions about the size of republics on their head. Instead of trying to keep the republics small and homogeneous, Madison seized on and ingeniously developed David Hume's radical suggestion that a republican government operated better in a large territory than in a small one. The republic, said Madison, had to be so enlarged, "without departing from the elective basis of it," that "the propensity in small republics to rash measures and the facility of forming and executing them" would be stifled. In a large republican society "the people are broken into so many interests and parties, that a common sentiment is less likely to be felt, and the requisite concert less likely to be formed, by a majority of the whole."[21] Madison and the other Federalists, in other words, accepted the reality of diverse competing partial interests in American politics and were quite willing to allow them free play.

But Madison was not a modern-day pluralist. He did not expect the new federal government to be neutralized into inactivity by the competition of these numerous diverse interests. Nor did he see public policy or the common good emerging naturally from the give-and-take of these clashing interests. He did not expect the new national government to be an integrator and harmonizer of the different interests in the society; instead he expected it to be a "disinterested and dispassionate umpire in disputes between different passions and interests in the State."[22] And it would do so because the men holding office in the new central government would by their fewness of numbers be more apt to be disinterested gentry who were not involved in the interest-mongering of the marketplace.

The new central government would combine the best of monarchy and republicanism. In monarchies the king was sufficiently neutral toward his subjects but often he sacrificed their happiness for his personal avarice or ambition. In small republics the government had no selfish will of its own, but it was never sufficiently neutral toward the various interests of the society. What the new extended republic would do, said Madison, was combine the good qualities of each. The new government would be "sufficiently neutral between the different interests and factions, to controul one part of the Society from invading the rights of another, and at the same time sufficiently controuled itself, from setting up an interest adverse to that of the whole society."[23]

In other words, Madison was willing to allow ordinary people to pursue their partial selfish interests in the expectation that they would be so diverse and clashing that they would rarely be able to combine into tyrannical majorities. This competitive situation would then allow those with "enlarged" and "liberal" outlooks to dominate government and promote the common good. It seemingly had worked that way in American religion, which was a common analogy for Madison. The multiplicity of religious sects in America prevented any from dominating the state and permitted the enlightened reason of philosophes like Jefferson and himself to shape public policy and church-state relations. "In a free government," wrote Madison in *The Federalist*, "the security for civil rights must be the same as that for religious rights. It consists in the one case in the multiplicity of interests, and in the other in the multiplicity of sects."[24]

This was one way in which Antifederalist arguments forced the Federalists to think freshly about politics and republican government. But as important and innovative as Madison's notion of an enlarged and elevated republic was, it did not match in originality and power, in sheer intellectual creativity, what the Federalists did with the idea of the sovereignty of the people.

The Antifederalists compelled the investigation of sovereignty by charging that the Constitution created what they called a consolidation, an eventual weakening if not destruction of the separate state governments. "The question turns," declared Patrick Henry at the opening of the Virginia ratifying convention, "on that poor little thing—the expression, We, the *people,* instead of the states, of America." "States," said Henry, "are the characteristics and soul of a confederation. If the states be not the agents of this compact, it must be one great consolidated, national government, of the people of all the states." Other Antifederalists agreed. "Instead of being thirteen republics, under a federal head," wrote the "Federal Farmer," the Constitution "is clearly designed to make us one consolidated government." The separate states would sooner or later succumb to the centralizing authority of the new national government.[25]

What gave power to these Antifederalist arguments that the proposed national government would inevitably end in a consolidation was the conventional eighteenth-century British theory of sovereignty. This was the notion expressed over and over during the debate between Britain and the colonies in the 1760s and 1770s—that in every state there had to be one final, indivisible, and incontestable lawmaking authority to which all other authorities must be ultimately subordinate. When Britain claimed that this supreme lawmaking authority lay in Parliament and the colonies in 1774 said that it lay in their separate colonial legislatures, the issue that would break the empire was drawn. The doctrine of sovereignty was the most important conception of politics in the eighteenth-century Anglo-American world, and it dominated the polemics of the entire Revolutionary generation from the moment in the 1760s when it was first raised through the adoption of the federal Constitution of 1787.

So when the Antifederalists in 1787–88 declared that there could be but one supreme legislative power in every state, they were invoking the logic of the best political science of the day. "I never heard of two supreme co-ordinate powers in one and the same country before," said Antifederalist William Grayson of Virginia, "I cannot conceive how it can happen." It was impossible, wrote Robert Yates of New York, that "the powers in the state constitution and those in the general government can exist and operate together." The logic of sovereignty demanded that either the state legislatures or the national Congress must predominate. There could be no compromise: "It is either a federal or a consolidated government, there being no medium as to kind."[26]

And the Antifederalists had no doubt that the federal government under the proposed Constitution, with its great sweeping power and its "supreme law of the land" authority, "must eventually annihilate the independent sovereignty of the several states." How long, the Antifederalists asked, would the people "retain their confidence for two thousand representatives who shall meet once in a year to make laws for regulating the height of your fences and the repairing of your roads?" Once the Constitution was established, "the state governments, without object or authority, will soon dwindle into insignificance, and be despised by the people themselves."[27] This conclusion was dictated, the Antifederalists said, by the logic of the doctrine of sovereignty.

The Antifederalists had a formidable argument. And the Federalists were hard put to deal with it. Some devout nationalists were willing to concede the Antifederalists' fears of the logic of sovereignty, but most Federalists, more politically sensitive, were aware that the American people would not accept the swallowing up of the states. After all, those who had been at the Philadelphia Convention had seen even strong nationalists like William Paterson of New Jersey balk at the extreme consolidation expressed in the Virginia Plan. Federalists realized that they would have to answer the Antifederalist charges that sovereignty—final, incontestable lawmaking power—would inevitably pass to the national government or lose the argument and with it the Constitution.

At first the Federalists tried to evade, refine, or deny the concept of sovereignty. They attempted to delineate "joint jurisdictions" and "coequal sovereignties" and to work out some way of sharing sovereignty between the national and state governments. But such efforts were doomed to fail. The idea that there must be in every state one supreme final lawmaking power was too firmly entrenched in eighteenth-century thinking to be denied or avoided.[28]

In the end it was left to James Wilson in the Pennsylvania ratifying convention to find the best answer to the Antifederalist arguments. More boldly and originally than anyone else, Wilson developed the position that became the basis of all Federalist thinking; indeed, it eventually became the basis of all thinking about

American government. Wilson challenged the Antifederalist case for the logic of sovereignty not by attempting to divide sovereignty or to deny it altogether, but by locating that power "from which there is no appeal, and which is therefore called absolute, supreme and uncontrollable"[29] only in the people at large. It seems a simple solution, but it was not, and its implications were enormous.

Sovereignty exists, conceded Wilson, but it cannot be located in either the federal government or the state legislatures; "it *resides* in the PEOPLE, as the fountain of government." The people never give up this sovereignty; it always stays with them. "They can delegate it in such proportions, to such bodies, on such terms, and under such limitations, as they think proper." Thus the people give some of their power to the institutions of the national government, some to the various state governments, and some at other extraordinary times to constitutional conventions for the specific purpose of making or amending constitutions. But unlike the British people in relation to their Parliament, the American people never surrender to any political institution or even to all political institutions together their full and final sovereign power. Always they retain their rights and their ultimate authority. Wilson was not saying, as men had for ages, that all governmental power was *derived* from the people. Instead he was saying that all government was only a temporary and limited agency of the people—out, so to speak, on a short-term, always recallable, loan. This was the principle underlying the new system, Wilson told the delegates in the Pennsylvania ratifying convention, and unless we grasp it, we shall never be able to understand how the people "may take from the subordinate governments powers with which they have hitherto trusted them, and place those powers in the general government."[30]

Although no Federalist seized and wielded this principle of the sovereignty of the people with more authority than Wilson, other Federalists in the ratification debates were inevitably pressured by persistent Antifederalist references to consolidation into invoking the same principle. Indeed, once Madison, Hamilton, and other Federalists saw the political and intellectual advantages of locating sovereignty in the people as a whole, they could scarcely restrain their excitement. Now they had a ready-made justification both for the Philadelphia Convention's bypassing the Confederation Congress and for the reliance on special state conventions in place of the state legislatures as instruments of ratification. Only by conceiving of sovereignty literally remaining with the people could the Federalists explain the emerging idea of federalism, where, contrary to the prevailing thought of the eighteenth century, both the state and national legislatures were equally representative of the people at the same time, "both possessed of our equal confidence—both chosen in the same manner, and equally responsible to us."[31]

Thinking about government and political power would never again be the same. Suddenly the Federalists saw all the fumbling efforts of Americans since the Revolution to create constitutions and governments in a new and clearer light. All the diverse and hitherto unrelated institutions and procedures that Americans had fashioned since 1776 now fell into place and were made into a meaningful whole. The Federalists now realized that government in America was different from government anywhere else in the world. It was not something that belonged to a king, a consul, a duke, a ruler, or any group of rulers whatsoever. For Americans there could be no preexisting rights of government adhering in anyone, no prerogative powers that the people had to bargain with and try to limit. In America, the Federalists concluded in wonderment at their own audacity, there no longer existed the age-old, seemingly permanent, distinction between rulers and ruled. Almost at a stroke the Federalists created the theoretical basis for all modern democracy.

With all sovereignty resting with the people the Federalists now saw that a constitution in America could no longer be regarded as it still was in England, as a contract or agreement between two hostile parties, between rulers and people. In America a constitution was not a charter of liberty granted by power but a charter of power granted by liberty. For Americans Magna Carta and the 1688 Bill of Rights were not constitutions at all. They "did not," wrote Thomas Paine, "create and give powers to Government in the manner a constitution does."[32] In America the people created constitutions and governments. They temporarily granted some of their power to their governmental agents, and these agents were now diverse and many. No longer were the people represented exclusively in the houses of representatives. All parts of America's governments—senates, governors, Congress, the president, yes, even judges at both the national and state level, could now intelligibly be described as the limited agents of the people. Government was simply the aggregation of the people's parcelled-out power, and all parts and all levels of this aggregate government were in some sense equally representative of the people.

There is no minimizing the significance of the Federalists' intellectual achievement hammered out in the heat of the struggle over the Constitution. It created a new realistic appreciation of the behavior of social groups and interests in politics and laid the basis for all subsequent American thinking about politics. Of course some Americans continued to talk about government and politics in traditional terms, in terms of compacts between rulers and ruled, in terms of embodying and balancing social estates in institutions of government. And the logic of the new Federalist thinking was not drawn out all at once. Indeed, we have had to wait nearly two centuries for some of the implications of the Federalist thinking to be fully realized. For example, only in the 1960s in its reapportionment decisions did the Supreme Court finally decide that the various state senates were as much agents of the people as the lower houses of representatives and thus electable only on the principle of "one person, one vote."

Still, despite the persistence of some traditional thinking well into the nineteenth century and some lingering relics of older assumptions even into our own time, what impresses about the intellectual achievement of 1787–88 is the rapidity with which it swept through the American mind and changed forever the discussion of American politics. Separation of powers, checks and balances, constitutions, limited government, all almost at once took on their modern meanings. With all governmental institutions being regarded as the people's limited agencies, the older identification of liberty as participation in government with liberty as the rights of individuals was broken. And the modern distinction between what has been called positive and negative liberty was born. In America it now became virtually impossible to think of liberty except as the rights of individuals standing against the government.

Like all ideologies these ideas born in the polemics over the Constitution quickly transcended the particular intentions of their creators. The Federalists, or the best of them, always tried to make theoretical sense of what they said and they always acted as if their audience was more than just those of their own time and place. Thus, despite the haste and urgency with which they often spoke and wrote, the monumental significance of their intellectual achievement was almost immediately grasped. And because these Federalist ideas were so popularly based and embodied what Americans had been groping toward from the beginning of their history, they were easily adopted and expanded by others with quite different interests and aims at stake. Indeed, in time they contributed to the destruction of the very classical aristocratic world of disinterested leisured gentry leadership the Federalists had sought to maintain. What began as Federalist political polemics ended as American political theory. It was theory of an importance unequaled in our history. That is why we Americans continue to regard the Federalists as something other than ordinary political statesmen. They are truly our "Founders."

Notes

1. *Federalist* 10:84.

2. Herbert J. Storing, ed., *The Complete Anti-Federalist*, 7 vols. (Chicago: University of Chicago Press, 1981), 1:28. See *Federalist* 15:107 for Hamilton's discussion of "the imbecility" of the Confederation government.

3. Max Farrand, ed., *The Records of the Federal Convention of 1787*, rev. ed., 4 vols. (New Haven: Yale University Press, 1966), 3:14 [hereafter referred to as Farrand, *Records*].

4. James Madison to Thomas Jefferson, October 17, 1788, Julian Boyd, ed., *The Papers of Thomas Jefferson*, 20 vols. (Princeton: Princeton University Press, 1950–55), 14:19.

5. Madison to George Washington, December 24, 1786, Robert A. Rutland et al., eds., *The Papers of James Madison*, 14 vols. (Chicago: University of Chicago Press, 1975), 9:225. On Madison's experience in the Virginia Assembly, see Gordon S. Wood, "Interests and Disinterestedness in the Making of the Constitution," in Richard Beeman et al., eds., *Beyond Confederation: Origins of the Constitution and American National Identity* (Chapel Hill: University of North Carolina Press, 1987), 73–75.

6. *Federalist* 10:79.

7. Madison to Jefferson, October 24, 1787, Boyd, *Papers of Thomas Jefferson*, 12:276.

8. *Federalist* 10:83.

9. Madison to Washington, April 16, 1787, Rutland et al., *Papers of James Madison*, 9:384.

10. Adam Smith, *An Inquiry into the Nature and Causes of the Wealth of Nations*, ed. Ernest Rhys, 2 vols. (London: J. M. Dent; New York: E. P. Dutton, 1910), vol. 2, bk. 5, chap. 1, pt. 3, art. 2, "Of the Expense of the Institutions for the Education of Youth," p. 249, and vol. 1, bk. 1, chap. 11, "Conclusion of the Chapter," p. 230.

11. *Federalist* 35:215, 216.

12. Ibid., 10:82, 83.

13. Storing, *Complete Anti-Federalist*, 1:51.

14. *Providence Gazette*, January 5, 1788.

15. Farrand, *Records*, 2:278; Jonathan Elliot, ed., *The Debates in the Several State Conventions on the Adoption of the Federal Constitution*, 2d ed., 5 vols. (Philadelphia: J. B. Lippincott, 1901), 2:256 [hereafter referred to as Elliot, *Debates*].

16. *Federalist* 39:240; 1:36.

17. Elliot, *Debates*, 3:222.

18. "Agrippa" Letters, in Paul L. Ford, ed., *Essays on the Constitution of the United States* (Brooklyn, N.Y.: Historical Printing Club, 1892), 64–65.

19. *Federalist* 10. See Madison to Jefferson, October 14, 1787, Boyd, *Papers of Thomas Jefferson,* 12:277–78; Farrand, *Records,* 1:214.

20. *Federalist* 10:80.

21. Farrand, *Records,* 2:204; Madison to Jefferson, October 24, 1787, Boyd, *Papers of Thomas Jefferson,* 12:277–78; *Federalist* 10. See Douglass Adair, " 'That Politics May Be Reduced to a Science': David Hume, James Madison, and the Tenth *Federalist," Huntington Library Quarterly* 20 (1956–57): 343–60.

22. Madison to Washington, April 16, 1787, Rutland et al., *Papers of James Madison,* 9:384.

23. Madison, "Vices of the Political System of the United States," in ibid., 9:357.

24. *Federalist* 51:324.

25. Elliot, *Debates,* 3:44; Letters from a Federal Farmer, in Paul L. Ford, ed., *Pamphlets on the Constitution of the United States* (Brooklyn, N.Y.: Historical Printing Club, 1888), 282.

26. Elliot, *Debates,* 3:281; [Robert Yates] "Sidney, I." June 13, 1788, in Paul L. Ford, ed., *Essays on the Constitution of the United States* (Brooklyn, N.Y.: Historical Printing Club, 1892), 304; Philadelphia, *Independent Gazetteer,* April 15, 1788, in John B. McMaster and Frederick D. Stone, eds., *Pennsylvania and the Federal Constitution 1787–88* (Lancaster, Pa.: Inquirer Printing and Publishing, 1888), 535.

27. Elliot, *Debates,* 2:312–13.

28. James Madison, in ibid., 3:381.

29. McMaster and Stone, *Pennsylvania and the Federal Constitution,* 229.

30. James Wilson, December 4, 1787, Pennsylvania Convention Debate, in ibid., 316, 302.

31. Elliot, *Debates,* 3:301.

32. Thomas Paine, *The Rights of Man,* in Philip S. Foner, ed., *The Life and Writings of Thomas Paine* (New York: Citadel Press, 1945), 382.

P eter S. Onuf was born in 1946, in New Haven, Connecticut. Now a
professor of history at Southern Methodist University, he has also
taught at the University of California at San Diego, Columbia University, and Worcester Polytechnic Institute. He went to Johns Hopkins
University, where he received his A.B. (1967) and Ph.D. (1973). His
doctoral dissertation, written under Jack P. Greene, was revised and
published as *The Origins of the Federal Republic* (Philadelphia: University
of Pennsylvania Press, 1983). Here Onuf argues that jurisdictional controversies within and among states in the 1770s and early 1780s helped
shape American notions about federalism and union. As states attempted to define their sovereignty as well as that of the new nation,
some leaders advocated a stronger central government to control what
they saw as dangerously divisive state and sectional differences. Onuf's
emphasis on the mix of interest and ideology in Revolutionary America
is likewise reflected in numerous articles and in his recent history of the
Northwest Ordinance, *Statehood and Union* (Bloomington: Indiana University Press, 1987).

Professor Onuf has shown that the desire to expand and the competition between states over what should be done with western lands in part
determined the course of national politics. Regional differences as well
as state rivalries within the same region therefore figure prominently in
his arguments. In the following pages he discusses the ideas of those in
the 1780s who not only felt that the Articles of Confederation were
inadequate, but who also believed that the nation would be better off if
it split into several separate republics. Such thinking, he contends, was
a logical, intermediate step between the ideas about nationhood and
sovereignty embodied in the Articles of Confederation and what would
come with the Constitution. Champions of the Constitution countered
with their appeal to "enlightened self-interest."

II

CONSTITUTIONAL POLITICS: STATES, SECTIONS, AND THE NATIONAL INTEREST

★

Peter S. Onuf

Ideally the federal Constitution would create "a more perfect Union." But was a stronger central government compatible with the "Union" most Americans cherished? Federalists insisted that the union was more than a league of distinct, sovereign states, dedicated simply to collective security. As long as the states continued to control the central government, the union would remain radically imperfect and all efforts to amend the Articles of Confederation were bound to fail. Under the existing, "imbecilic" system, they argued, the true national interest could never be effectively promoted—or even recognized.

But proponents of constitutional reform had to overcome formidable obstacles. It was easy enough for them to demonstrate the defects of the Confederation Congress; it was much more difficult to redefine "union" in a way that would rationalize the new regime's redistribution of power. Federalists had to persuade skeptical voters that a transcendent national interest really existed, while reassuring them that the price of a more "energetic" government would not be the loss of individual liberties or states' rights.

The authors of the Articles that were sent out to the states in 1777 and finally ratified in 1781 had been determined not to recreate the tyrannical central authority that had driven the colonists to revolution. According to Article II, "Each state retains its sovereignty, freedom, and independence": this union would be based on consent, not coercion. During the war, the states cooperated effectively, recognizing the central role of Congress and the Continental Army in vindicating American rights and securing the benefits of self-government. For enthusiastic Revolutionaries, union as means converged with union as end: because republican citizens and states were naturally drawn to each other, the elimination of Britain's corrupting rule would usher in a millennium of harmony and peace.

Yet, proponents of the new Constitution insisted, such a voluntaristic and consensual "union" had proven inadequate to the exigencies of the postwar period. Furthermore, the tendency to think of union in these terms worked against the institution of a more energetic government, capable of enforcing its will across the continent. Any real or imagined threat to particular rights or interests could be resisted on principled grounds for violating the true spirit of the union. The challenge to reformers was to show that their proposed system was compatible with the genius of American politics: they had to convince voters that the American union would not be destroyed, but would instead be made more "perfect" under the Constitution. Without abandoning the revolutionary commitment to republican liberty, reformers promoted a new conception of the union grounded in a more substantial idea of the national interest.

ENLIGHTENED SELF-INTEREST

In April 1787 a Boston writer lamented the disjointed state of the union:

> We are no longer United States, because we are not under any form of energetic compact. The breath of jealousy has blown the cobweb of our confederacy asunder. Every link of the chain of union is separated from its companion. We live it is true under the appearance of friendship, but we secretly hate and envy, and endeavour to thwart the interest of each other.

As this writer saw it, the nation had been reduced to the tattered remnants of a defensive league, held together more by "a principle of fear" than by a common commitment to republican liberty. Now that the war was over, he continued, many Americans believed that elaborate collective security arrangements were unnecessary. Congress, as a result, was on the verge of collapse. But Americans would be foolish to rely on the spontaneous revival of union in the event of future attacks, even if external threats, by enforcing union, had thus far kept the states from despoiling one another. Were "it not for the British colonies and garrisons that surround us," the Boston writer concluded, "we should probably very soon contend in the field for empire."[1]

The crucial rhetorical move in this essay was to suggest that the existing union was artificial, that it had been imposed on the states by the exigencies of the war. The union, another writer suggested, had been British, not American: "the English army" took the place of an American "executive" by forcing unified action; meanwhile "the zeal and fears of the people kept them in tolerable subordination" to Congress.[2] Even as American arms triumphed, the states remained dependent on Britain for whatever unity they enjoyed. British commentators recognized the reactive character of the American union, concluding that Britain would sooner achieve its goals of keeping the new nation weak by avoiding the battlefield and letting the Americans destroy one another.[3] Although the anticipated bloodbath had not yet occurred—and counterrevolution was thus delayed—many Americans were convinced by 1787 that the new nation's independence was jeopardized by the lack of an "energetic" central government.[4] The challenge was to create an authentically American union that could hold its own in a hostile world while enabling enterprising American citizens to pursue and achieve happiness.

Reformers advanced the paradoxical argument that a weak union had been sufficient during wartime but woefully inadequate since the peace. The "positive injunction of the law" was not necessary during the war, because the "interests" and "passions" of the people were easily mobilized "in the pursuit of an important object." But the *"acquisition"* and *"preservation"* of American independence were two different things.[5] "Such was the fervour of liberty and such the ready obedience of the people to slight recommendations," a New York essayist told the "Political

Freethinkers of America," that Congress had "formed a set of *faint rules*"—the Articles of Confederation—"which seemed rather to anticipate than to cement a federal combination." In the postwar period, however, as "America sat down in peace among the governors of the earth," the debilities of the union became increasingly obvious.[6] As Thomas Pownall, the former royal governor of Massachusetts, told his American friends in 1783, the American "Sovereign must now come forward amongst the Nations, as an active existing Agent."[7] Otherwise, the great gains of the Revolution would soon be forfeited as the new nation collapsed into disunion, anarchy, and counterrevolution.

Reformers portrayed the weak union under the Articles as unnatural. They emphasized the discrepancy between a general, popular commitment to national unity and political structures that effectively subverted it. Commenting on the "settlement of so many great Controversies" between the states, despite these inadequate structures, John Adams concluded that "the Union has great weight in the Minds of the People."[8] This attachment was not merely sentimental: the people identified their own interests with the interests of the nation as a whole. They recognized, a proponent of the new Constitution insisted, that the "true interests of the several parts of the Confederation are the same."[9] Federalists contrasted the naturalness of a more perfect union with the artificial state interests that now made the formulation of national policy—not to mention its execution—virtually impossible. In short, the nation was not represented in the present union. The result was the "novel" spectacle of a "numerous and encreasing people, and a boundless territory governed by a *committee of ways and means*," a potentially powerful and prosperous nation without a true government.[10]

Constitutional reformers mixed counsels of prudence—asserting that victory in the Revolution had not secured perpetual peace and that Americans must be ever ready to defend their independence—with paeans to the new nation's vast potential for economic development. An Albany writer thus proclaimed that the Constitution "will unite under one head, and bring to one point, the resources, strength and commerce of this country, and subsequently serve to render us wealthy, respectable, and powerful, as a mercantile as well as a warlike people."[11]

The Federalists' appeal to enlightened self-interest performed several important functions. First, they suggested that there was a positive, substantial national interest shared by all Americans, not just the small class of merchants, military men, and politicians who had taken such a prominent role in earlier efforts to strengthen the central government. The deterioration of national authority under the Articles thwarted enterprising Americans generally. The prospective interests of myriad citizens clearly transcended state boundaries, thus enabling Federalists to portray state sovereignty as an artificial barrier to popular enterprise. But most importantly, evocations of boundless prosperity enabled Federalists to develop a new conception of union and proclaim that its promise could only be fulfilled if a suitably effective national government was instituted.

The Federalist appeal to interest did not necessarily reflect a waning attachment to republican ideals, although this is what Antifederalists concluded.[12] Constitutional reformers had long argued that the habitual identification of narrow, selfish interests with republican principles gave both "principle" and "interest" a bad name. In fact, the pursuit of individual interest should serve the national interest, wrote "Lycurgus"—provided "the sentiments of mind bear some proportion to the objects surrounding it." True patriots, he suggested, were both visionary and practical enough to exploit nature's gifts: "The works of nature are certainly much superior in this country to those in any other that has yet been discovered."[13] "Cato" also emphasized the importance of developing the continent's natural advantages for "national happiness and respectability." Unfortunately, too many Americans were "influenced by partial and incomplete notions of civil and political liberty," and believed that "our deliverance from Britain" was a sufficient guarantee of the nation's welfare. Their mistake, "Cato" explained, was to juxtapose private interest and public good, thus rendering "liberty" a principle of mutual suspicion rather than collective enterprise. But "private happiness" and the "glory and security" of society were reciprocal:

> The idea that union is the assurance of private security, has induced [individuals] not only to unite, but to feel a most sensible interest in the safety of the state, its dignity, its capacity and power. It is a general principle that this concern, this attachment to one's country, results from an ardent and active desire of

private safety and happiness: If this be not true, Patriotism is an inexplicable affection, founded on no human principles, and embracing a visionary and fantastical object. [14]

Misguided republicans who preached austerity and self-denial rejected nature's gifts and undermined the foundations of social union. This false opposition of liberty and union obstructed every effort to resuscitate the feeble Congress, dividing and impoverishing the states and jeopardizing their independence.

Reformers sought to discredit the "partial and incomplete" notions of republican liberty that threatened to betray the new nation's dazzling promise. Always assuming the worst about each other and therefore unable to formulate effective national policies, Americans so far had squandered their natural advantages. As a result, "Observator" wrote, "our public, political interests, and with them individual interests (for they will stand or fall together) cannot be promoted, but must be neglected, and in the end inevitably ruined."[15] "Motives of self-interest" and "patriotism" thus converged, another writer agreed, in recommending the "radical cure" of a more powerful Congress that could regulate trade in the national interest and "counteract those illiberal and impolitic systems, whose influence, like that of a malignant comet, has operated so banefully throughout the states."[16] Only with the institution of an effective national government, "Observator" concluded, would it be possible to unite the states in "one consistent plan of measures," and so "unite all the streams of water on the continent, and confine them in one channel."[17]

NATIONALISM AND SECTIONALISM

Appeals to enlightened self-interest suggested an attractive new conception of union. But, as Federalists acknowledged when they distinguished "real" from "apparent" interests, different definitions of interest could lead in different directions. Antifederalists were not convinced that "the people of the United States have one common interest" or that the integrated development of the continent's resources was somehow decreed by nature.[18] If "interest is the band of social union," Timothy Bloodworth told the North Carolina ratifying convention, the American union could not long survive. Dismissing fanciful visions of future harmony and boundless prosperity, Bloodworth drew attention to the existing array of "jarring interests"—the differences in "soil, climate, produce, and every thing"—that divided "the Eastern, Southern, and the Middle States."[19] In view of such differences, any augmentation of national power was bound to benefit one section at the others' expense.

In the years leading up to the Philadelphia Convention, advocates of regional interests pushed for more effective national regulation and joined in disparaging state particularism. Discordant state policies subverted the effective defense or promotion of sectional interests. At the same time, however, intersectional conflict raised concern about the potential abuse of national power should one section or another gain control of Congress. Thus, although many leading politicians throughout the country were apparently united in bemoaning the excesses of the states, their growing awareness of distinctive regional interests threatened to preclude any coordinated response to the looming "crisis." Because the present government could not counter these centrifugal tendencies, the union was in danger of collapsing.

Impasse in Congress meant inaction, a Philadelphian wrote in 1785, even though "the necessities and opposite interests of the constituent states, brook no delay nor doubt." If Congress failed to respond to these demands, he warned, southerners, westerners, and northerners would undoubtedly take matters into their own hands and the union would be destroyed.

> Will the southern provinces, when in proper cultivation, wait the finger of Congress to point out markets for them?—Will the back settlers, adventurers and traders wait and languish upon a Spanish negociation, to give them the use of the Mississippi's stream, that washes their plantations? Will the eastern and northern states listen to the restrictions and prohibitions of Congress . . . ?[20]

The problem, many Americans began to fear, was that Congress could not help one set of interests without hurting another. The result was a deepening ambivalence about the desirability of a strong national government; the crucial question was whether or not sectional interests could be both protected and promoted in a more energetic union.

Because of the problematic relationship between conceptions of the national interest and this emerging sectional consciousness, agitation for constitutional reform threatened to destroy the union even as reformers promised to perfect it. When nationalists derided the present "imbecilic" system, they inevitably conflated their own interests with the national interest. But frustration with congressional impotence led some of these "nationalists" to betray their sectional biases. A Boston correspondent, for example, wondered how long we are "to continue in our present inglorious acquiesence in the shameful resistance that some of the states persist in, against federal and national measures?" He chafed at the "paltry politics, weak jealousy," and "local interests" of the middle states, concluding with a widely reprinted proposal that New England form a "new and stronger union" of its own.[21]

The great achievement of the Philadelphia Convention was to establish a framework for national politics that would accommodate these powerful sectionalist tendencies. It was easy enough to discredit the Articles of Confederation and lay the nation's troubles at the feet of state particularism; but the institution of a more powerful continental regime was not the only, or necessarily the most compelling, solution. In 1786 and early 1787, many commentators—articulating some of the same concerns that prompted national constitutional reform—had seriously considered the possibility of disunion. The controversy, contrary to later Federalist claims, did not pit benighted localists with their narrow conceptions of interest against cosmopolitans who could comprehend the new nation's magnificent prospects. Instead, proponents of radical constitutional change promoted ambiguous and contradictory conceptions of the national interest—and even of distinct national interests.

By the time of the Constitutional Convention, the belief that the United States might ultimately divide into three or more separate confederacies was widespread. The conventional projection was that the northern, middle, and southern states would form separate unions—and some saw the new states to the west constituting yet another union. In 1781 Alexander Hamilton predicted such a division in his *Continentalist* series: the "vanity and self importance" of "some of the larger states" might lead them "to place themselves at the head of particular confederacies independent of the general one."[22] Many British writers were convinced that the union would collapse after the war, including Richard Champion, who anticipated that "three great Republicks" eventually would emerge.[23] But it was only in 1786, in the wake of the Mississippi controversy, that American politicians seriously began to consider disunion. Writing from New York, Congressman James Monroe told his Virginia correspondents that northerners "have even sought a dismemberm[en]t to the Potowmack."[24] Although several division proposals did appear in northern papers at this time, northerners were not alone in considering the idea.[25] Many southerners blamed northern commercial interests for John Jay's ill-fated treaty and became convinced that their states would be better off on their own. During the ratification controversy, Monroe and his Antifederalist allies argued that disunion was preferable to a system that could easily "sacrifice the dearest interests of the Southern States."[26]

Northerners and Southerners who threatened each other with the destruction of the union reflected a pervasive sense that sectional differences were intractable. At the same time, constitutional reformers were becoming increasingly despondent about the prospects of ever being able to establish a more energetic continental government. As a result, the possibility of forming more perfect regional unions gained significant support. Benjamin Rush, a prominent nationalist, wrote Richard Price in England that "some of our enlightened men" had begun to "despair of a more complete union of the States in Congress" and were proposing to divide the union in three. "These confederacies they say will be united by nature, by interest, and by manners, and consequently they will be safe, agreeable and durable."[27] Clearly, Rush thought these "enlightened men" were not misled by narrow conceptions of local interest. It was precisely because they could take a broad view, considering "nature" and "manners" as well as "interests," that Rush's friends concluded that the United States included three incipient nationalities. In the event of disunion, the New Yorker "Lycurgus" wrote, "the religion, manners, customs, exports, imports and general interest" of each section would be "the same"; this "unanimity would render us secure at home, and respected abroad, and promote agriculture, manufactures, and commerce."[28]

Why should respectable nationalists flirt with disunionism? Some may have been more concerned with restraining the "democratic despotism" of the states than with creating a powerful national government.[29] Efforts to draft new state constitutions that could secure property and guarantee order had either been stymied or had failed to achieve the desired results. In Pennsylvania, republican opponents of the state constitution hoped a new national constitution would, as Rush later put it, "overset our state dung cart."[30] But there was no necessary connection between restraining the excesses of the states and creating a strong national union. When Rush wrote Price, the chances of revising the Articles looked slim, making the institution of new governments on the regional level correspondingly attractive.

Not surprisingly, many of the separate confederacy proposals circulating on the eve of the Convention sought to subordinate the states to more powerful unions. While "Lycurgus" thought the states could preserve "the same sovereignty and internal jurisdiction" they now enjoyed, most disunionists recognized the need to curb state particularism. A Boston writer linked disunion with a regional redefinition of federal-state relations that he hoped would ultimately lead to national constitutional reform. He thought it high time "to form a new and stronger union," but the work would be best begun by instituting "a new Congress, as the Representative of the nation of New-England," leaving the other states "to pursue their own imbecile and disjointed ways" until they learned "experimentally" the value of supporting a properly constituted union.[31] "Reason" had even less patience with the states: state sovereignty was the fundamental defect of American politics. Because "there can only be one sovereignty in a government," he wrote, the "notion . . . of a government by confederation between several independent States, and each retaining its sovereignty, must be abandoned, and with it every attempt to amend the present Articles of Confederation." The solution was to "distribute the States into three republics," thereby simultaneously dissolving the union and amalgamating the separate states. Separate confederations, he suggested, violated political logic as much as the existing confederation and would fall prey to the same centrifugal tendencies.[32]

Southerners also looked to regional unions for protection against untrammeled state power. "The doctrine of three Confederacies, or great Republics, has its' advocates here," Madison learned from a Virginia correspondent in August 1787. At least one prominent Virginian who embraced this doctrine had called for the "extinction of State legislatures" within each new union.[33] Madison himself favored neither the abolition of the states nor the breakup of the union, but—given his low esteem for the Henryite majority in the Virginia Assembly—he probably sympathized with "enlightened men" who thought new regional unions would solve their problems.[34]

There was considerable ambiguity about what to call these proposed regional governments. The use of the word "republic," in apposition to or in lieu of "confederation," strongly suggests that disunionists generally did not contemplate creating regional replicas of the existing union. No one would have claimed that the national government under the Articles was "republican," and this defect had always given the states' defiance of Congress an aura of legitimacy. But designating the sectional confederations "republics" would clearly establish their primacy over the states they included, a usage that anticipated the Federalists' bold use of "popular sovereignty" to legitimize the radical reallocation of power between the states and the national government.[35]

Advocacy of sectional "republics" that would subsume if not destroy the state republics also represented an important stage in the evolution of reformers' ideas about the possibility of preserving republican government over an "extended sphere." Disunionists agreed that there were limits to the size of republics, an argument Antifederalists subsequently used to great advantage. "Reason" acknowledged the "difficulty" of representing and reconciling "the national concerns of a people so numerous, with a territory so extensive," concluding that the executive arm would have to be strengthened to an extent incompatible "with the principles of a democratic form."[36] "All political writers of eminence agree," wrote "Lycurgus"—as did many Antifederalists after him—"that a republic should not comprehend a large territory."[37] In projecting these extended, regional republics, disunionists pushed Montesquieu's premises to their limits but did not abandon them. Certainly, the new unions would be much larger than the small republics the influential French theorist had endorsed; many of the individual states themselves were, by this standard, too large.[38] But proponents of separate unions thought them sufficiently homogeneous and still small enough to support republican governments, while avoiding the weaknesses endemic to small states. The existence of separate states, they suggested, simply obstructed the formulation and implementation of policy on behalf of the general—regional—interest.

SEPARATE UNIONS AND THE EXTENDED REPUBLIC

On the eve of the Philadelphia Convention, many Americans—including future Federalists as well as Antifederalists—shared misgivings about the size of the American union. According to conventional wisdom, a large state could only be preserved by despotic authority. Suspicious republicans thus detected monarchical tendencies in efforts to reinvigorate Congress and thereby transform the union into a consolidated state.

On the eve of the Convention, republican anxieties about incipient despotism were fueled by rumors that many Americans favored the reestablishment of monarchical government. Even staunch republicans became convinced that the return of monarchy was inevitable. They only hoped that the day would be postponed as long as possible and that when it came, Americans would be able to negotiate favorable terms with a new royal line.[39] Exasperated by repeated failures to enlarge Congress's powers, "many, very many wish to see an emperor at the head of our nation."[40] Without an effective national government, the union would fall apart and the new nation would soon be at the mercy of foreign predators. George Washington thought there had to be "lodged somewhere a power which will pervade the whole union in as energetic manner, as the Authority of the State Governments extend over the several States." Recognizing that the union itself had to become a "state," Americans asked themselves what kind of government would be most appropriate. Many concluded that monarchy alone could sustain "energetic" government across the continent. Some "respectable characters," reported Washington, "speak of a monarchical form . . . without horror."[41]

Historians have paid too little attention to the spread of monarchist sentiment or to proposals for the division of the union that circulated before the delegates convened in Philadelphia. By then many Americans had become convinced of the "imbecility" of the existing union as well as of the inadequacies of the states. Some, in turn, saw the creation of a continental monarchy or a division of the union as the only plausible alternatives. The Convention had to create "an efficient federal government," David Ramsay wrote Jefferson in April 1787, or "I fear that the end of the matter will be an American monarch or three or more confederacies."[42] If forced to choose between those alternatives, many "respectable characters" would agree with an anonymous "gentleman in Virginia" who "reprobate[d] the idea of a division of the States." "My opinion is, that America would be happier under the government of France, or the present Empress of Russia, than be divided according to that malevolent suggestion."[43] But Madison thought the "bulk of the people" would resist monarchy: they "will probably prefer the lesser evil of a partition of the Union into three more practicable and energetic governments."[44]

Supporters of continental monarchy were not necessarily enemies of republican liberty. Monarchists could argue that the best form of government for the union was an open question; indeed, if there was a latent form in the existing system—although this might be doubted—it was probably monarchical. Congress had exercised many of the British king's prerogatives, most notably over war and peace.[45] Furthermore, an American monarchy would be constitutionally limited and thus compatible with the preservation of republican government in the states. Monarchists suggested that what was best for the states might not be best for the continent as a whole. Even good republicans like James Wilson had to concede that the "extent" of the United States "*seems* to require the vigour of Monarchy."[46] Hamilton simply did not think "a Republican Government could be established over so great an extent." "The British Government was the best in the world," he told the delegates at Philadelphia, and "he doubted much whether any thing short of it would do in America."[47]

Whatever the merits of monarchical schemes, Madison and his fellow reformers knew they could not gain the broad popular approval so essential to the legitimacy of any new regime in America. The challenge was to create more energetic governments without abandoning republican forms. Perhaps this could only be done on the regional level: separate unions might avoid the dangers of large size—the tendency of large states to succumb to despotism—while curbing the democratic excesses characteristic of small states. At the same time, these unions would accommodate fundamental differences of sectional interest. Reformers might not doubt that there was a true national interest but they were increasingly doubtful that other Americans could recognize it. They feared that a union that attempted to embrace such self-consciously hostile interests was doomed to factional paralysis. Regional unions would at least facilitate a harmony of interests over fairly extended spheres, while precluding the debilitating conflicts of interest that fostered anarchy and shattered the unity of small republics.

The brief flirtation of some frustrated reformers with the idea of separate unions can be seen as a crucial step toward conceptualizing the extended republic. The first task in this project was to dissociate republican government from its exclusive association with the states. While they were unable to shake off the conventional assumption that a "state" as large as the union could only be governed despotically, some reformers did suggest that the "more practicable and energetic" regional unions could still be republics. Meanwhile, reformers warned that the tendency of individual states to claim sovereign powers jeopardized their republican character.[48] The preservation of republican government depended on instituting a more effective union that could guarantee peace among the states and protect them from foreign powers. Reformers usually had the "British Model" in mind when they advocated more energetic central administration, but they knew the "bulk" of the people had no stomach for another king. The result of this impasse—the apparently hopeless task of striking the delicate and precarious balance between monarchical and republican principles and reconciling energy and liberty on a continental scale—was to make separate unions seem a plausible alternative.

After the Constitution was drafted, reformers quickly distanced themselves from the idea of separate confederations. Federalists presented the new system as an answer to disunionist scenarios, which they attributed to their Antifederalist opponents. Federalist rhetoric suggests that the primary goal of the Convention was not so much to restrain the states from democratic excesses—the suggestion would have been impolitic—as to keep them from joining separate unions. Washington thought the *Federalist* essays an excellent "antidote" to the scribblings of those "who wish to see this Union divided into several Confederacies."[49] Marylander Charles Carroll asserted that if voters did not endorse the new Constitution, the union would crumble "into many distinct confederacies," with "wars, devastation, rapin[e], [and] hatred" the inevitable results.[50] Opponents of the proposed system welcomed this confusion, Federalists charged, because of the opportunities it would give "state demagogues" to seize power and promote their selfish interests.[51]

But Federalist charges are misleading. While some Antifederalists undoubtedly did come to the conclusion that separate confederations would be preferable to a single "consolidated" union, they forthrightly denied that this was their original intent. Indeed, the notion of a voluntary, harmonious union of republics articulated by Antifederalists like James Winthrop and John Francis Mercer during the ratification controversy bore little resemblance to the sectional unions proposed in 1786 and early 1787.[52] I am convinced that Federalists were in fact attacking—and thus disavowing—a constitutional solution that like-minded reformers had seriously considered when prospects for an effective continental scheme seemed dimmest. Their polemics disguised their own loss of faith in the union. Projecting disunionism on their opponents, Federalists proposed to resolve a crisis that, as proponents of separate confederacies, some of them may have helped precipitate.

FEDERALISM

"Local politics & diversity of interest will undoubtedly find their way into the [Constitutional] Convention," David Humphreys wrote. As a result, he expected "a serious proposal will be made for dividing the Continent into two or three seperate Governments."[53] Madison later insisted that the delegates never discussed the possibility, but it clearly was never far from their minds.[54] An awareness of intractable sectional differences was apparent in Edmund Randolph's early proposal for a triple executive with members "drawn from different portions of the Country"; he regarded the alternative, a unitary executive, "as the foetus of monarchy."[55] George Mason, a later opponent of the Constitution, also favored a three-man executive:

> If the Executive is vested in three persons, one chosen from the
> Northern, one from the Middle, and one from the Southern
> States, will it not contribute to quiet the minds of the people
> and convince them that there will be proper concern paid to
> their respective concerns? Will not three men so chosen bring

with them, into office, a more perfect and extensive knowledge of the real interests of this great Union?[56]

Voters must be persuaded, Mason warned, that enlarged national powers would not be exercised at their expense.

Yet such an explicit, constitutional recognition of sectional differences was more likely to arouse than to allay anxieties about the misuse of national power. "If three or more [executives] should be taken from as many districts," Pierce Butler argued, "there would be a constant struggle for local advantages."[57] The constitution of the executive mirrored the state of the nation. If there was a unitary, transcendent national interest, Butler suggested, a single executive was most appropriate; but if sectional interests were paramount, disunion probably made more sense than a divided executive. Later in the debates, Gouverneur Morris asked the crucial question: Was the alleged distinction between North and South "fictitious or real?" If "fictitious," he concluded, "let it be dismissed & let us proceed with due confidence"; if "real, instead of attempting to blend incompatible things, let us at once take a friendly leave of each other."[58]

The new Constitution could not recognize the preeminence of sectional distinctions without subverting the essential premise of national unity. At the same time, however, the new national government would have to secure vital local and regional interests, most conspicuously in the case of the large slaveholding and slave-importing states. The delegates discovered an answer to these apparently contradictory requirements during their protracted debates over representation in the national legislature. Through the complex scheme that incorporated the principle of proportional representation in one house and state equality in the other, divergent interests would be protected against hostile national majorities without being explicitly recognized. Controversial sectional issues were hardly neglected at Philadelphia, but delegates early on made the crucially important decision to suppress all traces of earlier disunionist proposals. The sections would have to achieve some sort of accommodation within a federal framework that explicitly secured the rights of the states, not the sections.

The Virginia Plan set the agenda for Convention debates. Advocates of opposing principles of representation were deeply divided and, for several frustrating weeks, no satisfactory compromise seemed possible. But the debate deflected attention away from conflicting sectional interests. Both sides were committed to national union, albeit on radically different terms. The result of the controversy was to persuade delegates that the impasse between large and small states—not sectional distinctions—constituted the most momentous obstacle to a strong national government.[59] At the same time, however, they knew that their failure to resolve the controversy over representation could well lead to disunion and the formation of separate confederacies. Madison and the large state "nationalists" were not above threatening the small states with disunion and obliteration.[60] Madison was so frustrated by their intransigence, historian Rosemarie Zagarri shows, that he was willing to raise the spectre of sectional conflict:

> The great danger to our general government *is the great southern and northern interests of the continent, being opposed to each other. Look to the votes in congress, and most of them stand divided by the geography of the country, not according to the size of the states.*[61]

Madison tried to persuade small-state delegates that the Virginia Plan was the safest possible arrangement for their constituents; because of their antagonistic—sectional—differences, there was no "real danger" the large states would act in concert.

Although the small states remained obdurate, Madison's speech did point the way toward the remarkably forthright intersectional negotiations that dominated the second half of the Convention.[62] Paradoxically, however, the precondition for such negotiations was an agreement on representation that did *not* reflect the "great" sectional interests but instead juxtaposed the interests of large and small states in the respective houses. Madison insisted that proportional representation was the defining principle of a truly national government. Small-state delegates replied that one section would thereby gain a dominant position in both houses, thus subverting prospects for continuing union. "Let not too much be attempted," warned Connecticut's Oliver Ellsworth, lest "all may be lost." Any representation scheme that would "deprive" the generally small northeastern states of equal suffrage in at least one house "was at once cutting the body [of America] in two."[63]

Large-state nationalists were forced to accept Ellsworth's premise that the government of the union would have to be "partly national" and "partly federal," a formula later embraced by "Publius" in the *Federalist*.[64] If this meant that the political power of the small states would be exaggerated, Madisonian logic suggested that the practical effects would be inconsequential: their interests were as disparate as those of the large states. At the same time, the complicated system of representation established under the "Connecticut Compromise" provided additional security for sectional interests—as well as for all the states *as states*. Coming from a large, centrally located state with strong interests in national commercial and territorial expansion, the Virginians could discount such safeguards. For them, the interests of the state, region, and nation *apparently* coincided. Opposition to the Virginia Plan exposed the limits of Virginian "nationalism," however, and, as Lance Banning shows, Madison's great achievement at the Virginia ratifying convention was to convince his countrymen that modifications of the Virginia Plan were not fatal to their interests.[65]

Virginians might complain that the new Constitution did not adequately recognize or secure their state's preeminent position in the union, but the "partly national," "partly federal" system did serve to mitigate intersectional tensions. One important reason for this was a crucial ambiguity about which section would enjoy the immediate advantage under the new scheme. Anticipated population shifts—toward the south and west—as well as confusion about the precise limits of the sections (would New York be aligned with the New England states and did the middle states constitute a distinct section?) made the implications of union for sectional conflict exceedingly problematic.[66] Staughton Lynd has shown that northerners and southerners alike could project expansive visions of regional development in plans for the opening of the Old Northwest. The West, in turn, was a mirror for broader conceptions of a stronger union promoting distinctive—although not necessarily mutually exclusive—regional interests.[67] The Framers' remarkable success in neutralizing sectional interest, or, perhaps more accurately, in redirecting its tendency from disunion and separate confederacies toward a stronger national regime, is apparent in the wildly divergent and contradictory assessments of the union's dangerous tendencies by Antifederalists in different parts of the country.[68] As opponents of the Constitution sought to coordinate their efforts, they necessarily focused on common concerns about the despotic, "consolidationist" tendency of the new federal government, implicitly conceding that it might indeed operate equally—if equally dangerously—on all parts of the union.

More immediately, once the Convention was committed to the Connecticut Compromise, delegates could begin to talk about sectional interests without directly questioning the future of the union or the presumption of a national interest. Even when they indulged in the most extravagant rhetoric, the desirability of intersectional accommodation was understood. Thus, while South Carolinian Pierce Butler asserted that the interests of the southern and eastern (northern) states were "as different as the interests of Russia and Turkey," he spoke in favor of compromise.[69] Indeed, the articulation of distinct interests was essential for fixing the "bargain among the Northern & Southern States" described by Gouverneur Morris: A simple majority in Congress could regulate trade—a concession to northern commerce—but no duties could be laid on exports and there would be no federal interference with the slave trade for another twenty years.[70] The Carolinians in particular engaged in a certain amount of bluster and bluff, but the delegates were clearly committed to compromise in the Convention's last weeks.

The history of intersectional negotiations at the Constitutional Convention is familiar. It is not generally recognized, however, that agreement on the representation issue provided a framework for articulating those interests that encouraged mutual concessions. In this sense, contemporary commentators were correct in emphasizing the primacy of the representation controversy. Although, as Madison noted, conflicts over other issues might have been more "important," they only became negotiable once the character of the new national legislature was established. Ellsworth, who had himself broached the possibility of disunion in response to the large-state insistence on proportional representation, became a leading advocate of compromise. The failure to reconcile sectional differences, he told the Convention in late August, would lead "probably into several confederations and not without bloodshed."[71] Guarantees of sectional interests would, in turn, constitute powerful incentives to support the new system.

The great discovery of nationalist reformers at Philadelphia was that the equal representation of the states and the recognition of state sovereignty—which many of them considered the original source of America's troubles—could provide the crucial measure of security that would reverse the tendency toward disunion expressed in proposals for separate confederacies. As Banning suggests for Madison, the Convention was a "learning process."[72] Pragmatic reformers became aware of the limits on national consolidation set by the vast array of conflicting interests represented at Philadelphia and by the delegates' determination to uphold what they deemed their own states' critical interests. They also had to recognize limits on their own "nationalism" dictated by their distinctive regional interests. Given the imperative of reconciling those interests—and facing the awful alternative of disunion—nationalists turned toward the states. Gouverneur Morris, for instance, persisted in considering equal state voting a "vicious principle" but realized that it could provide a vital security for the northern commercial states as population shifted southward.[73]

The genius of states' rights within the framework of a more energetic national union was to secure sectional interests without directly acknowledging their legitimacy and durability. Of course, as Paul Finkelman shows, these guarantees, particularly on slavery, were woven into the very fabric of the new system.[74] When slavery subsequently became the leading cause of intersectional conflict, the constitutional guarantees of slave interests would foster disunion, even as they had once made union possible. The Framers of the Constitution attempted to suppress sectional tensions by creating a more perfect—if fundamentally flawed—national union. Perhaps not surprisingly, given the Framers' reliance on federalism to counteract sectionalism, southerners finally sought to vindicate their rights and protect their interests by invoking states' rights.

THE NATIONAL INTEREST

"Whether the plans of the Southern, Eastern or Middle States succeed, never, in my opinion, ought to be known," Congressman Nathan Dane wrote from New York as the Convention met behind closed doors in Philadelphia.[75] Dane shared the perspective of delegates who saw these sectional divisions as the leading threat to union. But Federalist defenders of the new Constitution did not seek to minimize intersectional conflict; instead they emphasized the obstacles the Framers had had to overcome to secure the national interest. "A delicate and difficult contest arose," Hamilton told the New York Convention, and the delegates realized that "it was necessary that all parties should be indulged" by "compromise, or the convention must have dissolved without effecting anything."[76] Given the "different interests of the different parts of the union," Madison added, "it was impossible to consider the degree of concord that ultimately prevailed as less than a miracle."[77] The two ideas—"compromise" and "miracle"—were closely linked. Only an "omnipotent, omnipresent, & beneficent Ruler" could have enabled the delegates to look beyond their own narrow interests and prejudices.[78]

Federalists insisted that the "mutual concessions" and "mutual sacrifices" that enabled the Convention to reach agreement could never be repeated. "Such an instance of unanimity upon a great national object can scarcely be paralleled."[79] It was unlikely the states ever would be able to respond to the Antifederalist call for a second convention. If such a meeting were held, John Jay predicted, proponents of separate confederacies would gain the upper hand; in the meantime, "it will naturally be their policy rather to cherish than to prevent divisions."[80] The Convention's great, even "miraculous," achievement was to fashion the "delicate" compromises that growing sectional tensions had made so necessary—and yet so difficult to negotiate. The Antifederalists' opposition to the new scheme only served to accentuate sectional suspicions, thereby guaranteeing the failure of any further efforts to preserve the union.

The Federalist challenge was not to conceal the Convention's compromises, but rather to show that they bore equally on all the states. How could "such heterogenous materials" be formed into an equitable union?[81] Under the Articles, "equality" had been secured by the *weakness* of the national government: ambitious states could *not* exploit each other by gaining control of Congress.[82] Federalists had to show that a strong national government, with authority over individual citizens as well as the states, would sustain an equitable balance of power among the states while promoting their common interests. They made their case by juxtaposing the proposed system to what they insisted would be the inevitable results of inaction. This meant, ironically, that they aimed much of their rhetoric at the alternative arrangements—notably, the division of the union into separate confederacies—that frustrated reformers had begun to consider in the dark days before the Convention met.

By insisting that voters had to choose between the proposed Constitution and the formation of separate and hostile unions, Federalists suggested a definition of the national interest. Clearly, it was in the interest of potentially belligerent sections to reach a peaceful accommodation. Preserving the peace was an inestimable benefit—provided the national union did not permit one section to gain a permanent advantage over the others. "Equality," defined as the guarantee of vital state and regional interests, depended on a more perfect union and a strong national government. To secure these benefits, concessions on less vital interests were necessary: "the new government, constructed on the broad basis of equality, mutual benefits, and national good, is *not* calculated to secure a single state all her natural advantages."[83] A Connecticut Federalist thus disclaimed any ambition "to obtain a preeminence over one another." The states, he concluded, "are content to be established on an equal footing."[84]

The South Carolinians, both at the Convention and during the ratification debate, were clearest about their own interests as slaveowning planters and about the necessity of intersectional compromise. David Ramsay thought that northern concessions on slavery warranted reciprocal concessions on trade regulation. "Ought we to grudge them the carrying of our produce," he asked, "especially when it is considered, that by encouraging their shipping, we increase the means of our own defence?"[85] With their large slave population, Carolinians were not eager to abandon the union, even for a southern confederacy.[86] "Like ourselves," Virginia's Governor Randolph wrote, "they are diminished in their real force, by the mixture of an unhappy species of population." Vulnerable internally and externally—"two or more confederacies cannot but be competitors for power"—Randolph concluded that southerners "would be compelled to rest some where or other, power approaching near to military government."[87] The southern states "are so weak," said Charles Cotesworth Pinckney of South Carolina, "that by ourselves we could not form a union strong enough for the purpose of effectually protecting each other."[88] Some Virginians, reported John Blair Smith, were even convinced they would have to seek "a foreign alliance."[89]

In late 1786 and early 1787 separate confederacies might have seemed a distinctly preferable alternative to an imbecilic continental union dominated by quasi-sovereign states. After the Philadelphia Convention, however, Federalists portrayed the formation of separate unions as the awful, probably inevitable outcome of disunion. They thus suggested a crucial distinction between legitimate sectional interests that could be guaranteed in a continental union and a section's illegitimate ambition to assume a dominant position. Such ambitions reflected the same shortsighted and partial conception of "interest" that was expressed in proposals for breaking up the union. But an imbalanced union could not long survive, nor could regional unions determined to promote their separate interests coexist peacefully. It was therefore essential for all the states to forswear the illusory advantages of *dominance,* either within the union or in a destructive competition among unions. And this meant, concluded Robert Barnwell of South Carolina, that—within clearly defined constitutional limits—the divergent, sometimes conflicting interests that made up the union had to submit to the majority will. If national power was always suspect, Barnwell reasoned, "it went against uniting at all." "A majority must be somewhere, is most evident: nothing would be more completely farcical than a government completely checked."[90]

The Federalists' major achievement was to articulate a plausible conception of the national interest that did not depend on the destruction of the states. They warned that the separate unions sure to emerge with the failure of constitutional reform represented a much greater threat to the survival of the states than a more energetic continental union. In the event of disunion, large states would no longer be inhibited from extending their power at the expense of their small neighbors; because of their conflicting interests, regional blocs would be on a hostile footing and the inevitable militarization of American politics would subvert republican government.[91]

Counsels of prudence were balanced by promises of future prosperity and power in Federalist rhetoric. According to promoters of the new system, the different interests that now jeopardized union could be mobilized to serve the common good. The choice was between reciprocity, commercial exchange, and economic development on one hand and mutual suspicion, war, and poverty on the other. A Federalist writer elaborated on the alternatives:

every moment seems to create new matter which will be productive either of building up a great and boundless empire, or circumscribing scanty and narrow limits for the inhabitants of this country, suited only for savage chiefs or barbarous tyrants—the latter will be the consequence, should we reject the government offered for our acceptance.[92]

Americans could balance and harmonize their interests—and extend their freedom—by embracing a stronger union; disunion was a prescription for "tyranny" and a violation of the continent's "natural" destiny.

Federalists claimed that Americans could enjoy both security and opportunity under the Constitution. That the new government would preserve states' rights ("equal justice will be administered to each state"[93]) was crucial to their argument. From the new perspective of sectional division—precipitated by the Mississippi furor and subsequent talk about separate confederacies—the excesses of state sovereignty no longer seemed to be the central problem for reformers. Instead, the debates at Philadelphia taught them that a careful balance of state and central power could provide a framework for containing and redirecting sectionalist impulses. Their new idea of federalism thus brought into view a broadly appealing conception of union and of the national interest. Indeed, Federalists concluded, Americans could only preserve their state republics, pursue their individual interests, and exploit the magnificent natural resources of the continent if they instituted a strong national government.

Americans could thus, they hoped, mitigate if not resolve the conflicts of interest that once threatened to paralyze and destroy the union. But, as Antifederalist critics of the Constitution warned, sectional distinctions would not necessarily dissolve under the new dispensation. Indeed, the issue of Southern slavery— and its constitutional guarantees—ultimately found its solution only in the terrible destruction and slaughter of the Civil War. The idea of a substantial and expanding national interest that figured so prominently in Federalist rhetoric during the ratification controversy could not be sustained in the face of such extreme sectional polarization.

Notes

1. Item in *Massachusetts Sentinel,* April 11, 1787, in Merrill Jensen et al., eds., *The Documentary History of the Ratification of the Constitution,* 8 vols. to date (Madison: State Historical Society of Wisconsin, 1976–), 13:79. [The volumes in this set are not being published sequentially; eventually there will be fifteen.]

2. "To the Political Freethinkers of America," *New York Daily Advertiser,* May 24, 1787, in ibid., 13:113–15.

3. Leon Fraser, *English Opinion of the American Constitution and Government (1783–1798)* (New York: Columbia University Press, 1915), 31–43. For examples, see Lord Sheffield [John B. Holroyd], *Observations on the Commerce of the American States,* 2d ed. (London, 1783), 104–5; item in *Times* (London), January 29, 1785; "Sketches of the Present Times," *Times* (London), February 2, 1786.

4. The terms "energetic" and "energy"—either lacking under the Confederation or assured under the new Constitution—were employed repeatedly by prominent Federalists. For example, see *Federalist* 1:35–36, 15:108, 22:148, 23:152–57, 26:168, 37:224–26, and 70:423–27.

5. Item in *Pennsylvania Herald* (Philadelphia), May 9, 1787, in Jensen et al., *History of Ratification,* 13:96–97.

6. "To the Political Freethinkers."

7. T[homas] P[ownall], *A Memorial Addressed to the Sovereigns of America* (London, 1783), 129. On American foreign policy during this period see Felix Gilbert, *To the Farewell Address: Ideas of Early American Foreign Policy* (Princeton, N.J.: Princeton University Press, 1961); James H. Hutson, *John Adams and the Diplomacy of the American Revolution* (Lexington: University of Kentucky Press, 1980); Gerald Stourzh, *Benjamin Franklin and American Foreign Policy,* 2d ed. (1954; reprint, Chicago: University of Chicago Press, 1969); and Frederick W. Marks III, *Independence on Trial: Foreign Affairs and the Making of the Constitution* (Baton Rouge: Louisiana State University Press, 1973).

8. John Adams to John Jay, May 8, 1787, in *Documentary History of the Constitution of the United States,* 5 vols. (Washington, D.C.: Department of State, 1894–1905), 5:137.

9. Item in *American Herald* (Boston), October 1, 1787, in Jensen et al., *History of Ratification,* 13:285–86.

10. "To the Political Freethinkers."

11. Item dated October 31, 1787, *Albany Gazette,* November 1, 1787, in Jensen et al., *History of Ratification,* 13:523–24.

12. "Letters From the Federal Farmer," reprinted in Cecelia Kenyon, ed., *The Antifederalists* (Indianapolis: Bobbs-Merrill, 1966), esp. letter 3, at 218–21.

13. "Lycurgus," no. 1, *New-Haven Gazette,* February 16, 1786. See also David Ramsay, *An Oration on the Advantages of American Independence* (Charleston, 1778), excerpted in Wilson Smith, ed., *Theories of Education in Early America, 1655–1819* (Indianapolis: Bobbs-Merrill, 1973), 221–29, at 226, and the discussion in Peter S. Onuf, "Liberty, Development, and Union: Visions of the West in the 1780s," *William and Mary Quarterly* 43 (1986): 179–213.

14. "Cato," "To the Public," *New-Haven Gazette,* January 25, 1787.

15. "Observator," no. 1, *New-Haven Gazette,* August 25, 1785.

16. Item in *Pennsylvania Gazette* (Philadelphia), June 29, 1785.

17. "Observator," no. 1, *New-Haven Gazette,* August 25, 1785.

18. William Davie speech, North Carolina Convention, July 29, 1788, in Jonathan Elliot, ed., *The Debates in the Several State Conventions on the Adoption of the Federal Constitution,* 2d ed., 5 vols. (Philadelphia: J. B. Lippincott, 1901), 4:157–58 [hereafter referred to as Elliot, *Debates*].

19. Timothy Bloodworth speech, North Carolina Convention, July 28, 1788, in ibid., 134–35.

20. "Extract of a Letter from Philadelphia," n.d., *Columbian Herald* (Boston), July 11, 1785.

21. Item in *Independent Chronicle* (Boston), February 15, 1787, in Jensen et al., *History of Ratification,* 13:57. The editors have identified nineteen reprintings of this piece in ten states before May 12, 1787, ibid., 13:59n.

22. [Alexander Hamilton], "Continentalist," no. 3, August 9, 1781, in Harold C. Syrett, ed., *The Papers of Alexander Hamilton,* 26 vols. (New York: Columbia University Press, 1961–79), 2:660–61. Hamilton, Jay, and Madison all alluded to such talk of several confederacies in *The Federalist;* see, for example, 1:36, 2:37–41, 3:41, 5:51–53, 6:54, 7:64–65, 8:66–68, 9:71, 12:95, and 13:97–99.

23. Richard Champion, *Considerations on the Present Situation of Great Britain and the United States of America* (London, 1784), 238–39.

24. James Monroe to James Madison, September 3, 1786, in Edmund Cody Burnett, ed., *Letters of the Members of the Continental Congress,* 8 vols. (Washington, D.C.: Carnegie Institution, 1921–36), 8:462. On intersectional tensions in this period see Joseph L. Davis, *Sectionalism in American Politics, 1774–1787* (Madison: University of Wisconsin Press, 1977); Thomas P. Slaughter, *The Whiskey Rebellion: Frontier Epilogue to the American Revolution* (New York: Oxford University Press, 1986), 36–45 and passim; Drew R. McCoy, "James Madison and Visions of American Nationality in the Confederation Period: A Regional Perspective," in Richard Beeman et al., eds., *Beyond Confederation: Origins of the Constitution and American National Identity* (Chapel Hill: University of North Carolina Press, 1987), 226–58; Peter S. Onuf, *Statehood and Union: A History of the Northwest Ordinance* (Bloomington: Indiana University Press, 1987), chap. 3.

25. Editorial note, in Jensen et al., *History of Ratification,* 13:54–57.

26. Monroe speech, Virginia Convention, June 10, 1788, in Elliot, *Debates,* 3:221.

27. Benjamin Rush to Richard Price, October 27, 1786, in Lyman Butterfield, ed., *The Letters of Benjamin Rush,* 2 vols. (Princeton, N.J.: Princeton University Press, 1951), 1:408–10.

28. "Lycurgus," dated March 30, 1787, *New York Daily Advertiser,* April 2, 1787, in Jensen et al., *History of Ratification,* 13:58–59.

29. Gordon Wood, *The Creation of the American Republic, 1776–1787* (Chapel Hill: University of North Carolina Press, 1969), 409–13.

30. Rush to Timothy Pickering, August 30, 1787, in Butterfield, *Letters of Benjamin Rush*, 1:439–40. See also Rush speech, Pennsylvania Convention, December 3, 1787, in Jensen et al., *History of Ratification*, 2:457–58.

31. Item in *Independent Chronicle* (Boston), February 15, 1787, in Jensen et al., *History of Ratification*, 13:57.

32. "Reason," "A Thought for the Delegates to the Convention," *New York Daily Advertiser*, March 24, 1787, in ibid., 57–58; reprinted nine times in seven states by April 28.

33. James McClurg to Madison, August 5, 1787, in Robert A. Rutland et al., eds., *The Papers of James Madison*, 14 vols. (Chicago: University of Chicago Press, 1975), 10:134–36.

34. On James Madison's thinking in this period see the excellent essays by Lance Banning, including "The Practicable Sphere of a Republic: James Madison, The Constitutional Convention, and the Emergence of Revolutionary Federalism," in Beeman et al., *Beyond Confederation*, 162–87, and "Virginia: Nation, State, and Section," in Michael Lienesch and Michael Gillespie, eds., *Ratifying the Constitution* (forthcoming).

35. Wood, *Creation of the American Republic*, 530-36.

36. See the discussion in Cecelia Kenyon, "Men of Little Faith: The Antifederalists on the Nature of Representative Government," reprinted in Jack P. Greene, ed., *The Reinterpretation of the American Revolution* (New York: Harper and Row, 1968), 526–66, at 529–33. According to the Antifederalist "Cato," "the extent of many of the states of the Union, is at this time almost too great for the superintendence of a republican form of government." *New York Journal*, October 25, 1787, in Paul L. Ford, ed., *Essays on the Constitution of the United States* (Brooklyn, N.Y.: Historical Printing Club, 1892), 255–59, at 258.

37. "Reason."

38. "Lycurgus."

39. Louise Burnham Dunbar, *A Study of "Monarchical" Tendencies in the United States from 1776 to 1801* (Urbana: University of Illinois Press, 1922); editorial note, in Jensen et al., *History of Ratification*, 13:168–72.

40. Item in *American Museum* (March 1787), in ibid., 76–77.

41. George Washington to John Jay, August 1, 1787, in *Documentary History of the Constitution*, 5:19–21 [full citation at note 8].

42. David Ramsay to Thomas Jefferson, April 7, 1787, in ibid., 109.

43. "Extract of a letter from a gentleman in Virginia," *Independent Gazetteer* (Philadelphia), June 26, 1787, in Jensen et al., *History of Ratification*, 13:145–47.

44. Madison to Edmund Pendleton, February 24, 1787, in Rutland et al., *Papers of James Madison*, 9:294–96.

45. Peter S. Onuf, *Origins of the Federal Republic: Jurisdictional Controversies in the United States, 1775–1787* (Philadelphia: University of Pennsylvania Press, 1983), 7, 16.

46. James Wilson speech, June 1 (King notes), in Max Farrand, ed., *The Records of the Federal Convention of 1787*, rev. ed., 4 vols. (New Haven, Conn.: Yale University Press, 1966), 1:71 (emphasis added) [hereafter referred to as Farrand, *Records*].

47. Hamilton speech, June 18, in ibid., 288.

48. Peter S. Onuf, "State Sovereignty and the Making of the Constitution," in Terence Ball and J. G. A. Pocock, eds., *Conceptual Change and the Constitution* (Lawrence: University Press of Kansas, 1988), 79–98.

49. George Washington to Dr. Stuart, November 30, 1787, in *Documentary History of the Constitution*, 5:382–84.

50. Edward C. Papenfuse, "An Undelivered Defense of a Winning Cause: Charles Carroll of Carrollton's 'Remarks on the Proposed Federal Constitution,' " *Maryland Historical Magazine* 71 (1976): 220–51, at 250.

51. Henry Knox letter [September 1787], in Jensen et al., *History of Ratification*, 13:279–80.

52. For the Antifederalist idea of union see James Winthrop's "Agrippa" letters, collected in Ford, *Essays on the Constitution*, 44–122, and the letters of "Farmer" (probably John Francis Mercer), in Herbert J. Storing, ed., *The Complete Anti-Federalist*, 7 vols. (Chicago: University of Chicago Press, 1981), 5:5–78. Also see the discussion in Onuf, "State Sovereignty."

53. David Humphreys to George Washington, April 9, 1787, in *Documentary History of the Constitution*, 5:109–10.

54. Madison to Jefferson, October 24, 1787, in Rutland et al., *Papers of James Madison*, 10:205–20, at 207.

55. Edmund Randolph speeches, June 2 and 1 (Madison notes), in Farrand, *Records*, 1:88, 66.

56. George Mason speech, June 4 (Mason notes), in ibid., 113.

57. Pierce Butler speech, June 2 (Madison notes), in ibid., 88–89.

58. Gouverneur Morris speech, July 13 (Madison notes), in ibid., 604.

59. Rosemarie Zagarri, *The Politics of Size: Representation in the United States, 1776–1812* (Ithaca, N.Y.: Cornell University Press, 1987), chap. 3; Peter S. Onuf, "State Equality and a More Perfect Union," in Lienesch and Gillespie, *Ratifying the Constitution* [full citation at note 34].

60. Madison speech, June 19 (Madison notes), in Farrand, *Records*, 1:320–21.

61. Madison speech, June 29 (Yates notes), in ibid., 476; Zagarri, *Politics of Size*, chap. 3.

62. On the relative importance of questions of principle and interest and for a more elaborate account of the Convention's successive "phases," see Calvin Jillson and Thornton Anderson, "Realignments in the Convention of 1787: The Slave Trade Compromise," *Journal of Politics* 39 (1977): 712–29; Jillson, "Constitution-Making: Alignment and Re-alignment in the Federal Convention of 1787," *American Political Science Review* 75 (1981): 598–612; Jillson and Cecil Eubanks, "The Political Structure of Constitution Making: The Federal Convention of 1787," *American Journal of Political Science* 28 (1984): 435–58; Jillson, "Ideas in Conflict: Political Strategy and Intellectual Advantage in the Federal Convention," Herman Belz and Ronald Hoffman, eds., *To Form a More Perfect Union: The Critical Ideas of the Constitution* (forthcoming from University Press of Virginia.) For an excellent account of the representation controversy, see Jack N. Rakove, "The Great Compromise: Ideas, Interests, and the Politics of Constitution Making," *William and Mary Quarterly* 44 (1987): 424–57, and for a careful reconstruction of the various slavery compromises see Paul Finkelman, "Slavery and the Constitutional Convention: Making a Covenant with Death," in Beeman et al., *Beyond Confederation*, 188–225 [full citation at note 24].

63. Oliver Ellsworth speech, June 29 (Madison notes), in Farrand, *Records*, 1:469.

64. Ellsworth speech, June 29 (Madison notes), in ibid., 468; *Federalist* 39:246.

65. Banning, "Virginia: Nation, State, and Section" [full citation at note 34].

66. McCoy, "Madison and Visions of American Nationality," 235 [full citation at note 24]; John Richard Alden, *The First South* (Baton Rouge: Louisiana State University Press, 1961), chap. 1.

67. Onuf, "Liberty, Development, and Union," [full citation at note 13].

68. See "Federalism's" comments in *Maryland Journal* (Baltimore), May 9, 1788: Antifederalists "agree to oppose the proposed government, but no two sets of objectors, nay, no two objecting individuals . . . concur in making the same exceptions."

69. Butler speech, August 29 (Madison notes), in Farrand, *Records*, 2:457.

70. Morris speech, August 22 (Madison notes), in ibid., 374.

71. Oliver Ellsworth speech, August 22 (Madison notes), in ibid., 375.

72. Banning, "Practicable Sphere of a Republic," 178 [full citation at note 34].

73. Morris speech, July 13, 1787, in Farrand, *Records*, 1:604.

74. Finkelman, "Slavery and the Constitutional Convention."

75. Nathan Dane to Rufus King, June 19, 1787, in Farrand, *Records*, 3:48.

76. Hamilton speech, New York Convention, June 20, 1788, in Elliot, *Debates*, 2:236.

77. Madison to Jefferson, October 24, 1787, in Rutland et al., *Papers of James Madison*, 10:208–9.

78. Benjamin Franklin to the Editor of the *Federal Gazette*, April 8, 1788, in Farrand, *Records*, 3:296–97. See the discussion in Onuf, *Origins of the Federal Republic*, 207–9 [full citation at note 45].

79. Daniel Clymer speech, Pennsylvania Convention, September 28, 1787, in Jensen et al., *History of Ratification*, 2:76–77; "One of the People," *Pennsylvania Gazette*, October 17, 1787, in ibid., 191.

80. John Jay, *An Address to the People of New York* (New York, 1788), in Paul L. Ford, ed., *Pamphlets on the Constitution of the United States* (Brooklyn, N.Y.: Historical Printing Club, 1888), 67–86, at 82.

81. James Wilson's Speech in the State House Yard, October 6, 1787, in Jensen et al., *History of Ratification*, 2:167–72, at 170.

82. Patrick Henry speeches, Virginia Convention, June 7 and 9, 1788, in Elliot, *Debates*, 3:145, 151–52.

83. "Aristides" [Alexander Contee Hanson], *Remarks on the Proposed Plan of a Federal Government* (Annapolis, 1788), in Ford, *Pamphlets*, 217–57, at 255 (emphasis added).

84. "Observator," no. 5, *New-Haven Gazette*, September 20, 1787, in Jensen et al., *History of Ratification*, 3:348.

85. Ramsay, *An Address to the Freemen of South Carolina on the Subject of the Federal Constitution* (Charleston, [1788]), in Ford, *Pamphlets*, 371–80, at 377.

86. Edward Rutledge speech, January 17, 1788, and Charles Pinckney speech, May 14, 1788, South Carolina Convention, in Elliot, *Debates*, 4:299, 331–32.

87. Randolph, *Letter on the Federal Constitution*, October 10, 1787 (Richmond, 1787), in Ford, *Pamphlets*, 259–76, at 270.

88. Gen. C. C. Pinckney speech, South Carolina Convention, January 17, 1788, in Elliot, *Debates*, 4:283–84.

89. John Blair Smith to Madison, June 12, 1788, in Rutland et al., *Papers of James Madison*, 11:119–21.

90. Robert Barnwell speech, South Carolina Convention, January 17, 1788, in Elliot, *Debates*, 4:292–93.

91. Onuf, "State Sovereignty" [full citation at note 48].

92. Item in *Hampshire Gazette* (Northampton, Mass.), October 31, 1787, in Jensen et al., *History of Ratification*, 13:316.

93. Item dated October 31, 1787, *Albany Gazette*, November 1, 1787, in ibid., 523–24.

Lance Banning's work is often cited in discussions of political ideology in the early republic. Banning took his B.A. in 1964 from the University of Missouri, Kansas City, and earned a Ph.D. at Washington University seven years later. He taught in the American Civilization program at Brown University before moving to the University of Kentucky, where he is a professor of history.

At Washington University Banning studied with John Murrin and J. G. A. Pocock. Their influence is reflected in *The Jeffersonian Persuasion* (Ithaca, N.Y.: Cornell University Press, 1978), which began as Banning's doctoral dissertation. In it Banning traces the origins of Jeffersonian political ideology to seventeenth-century English Whigs like James Harrington. The Jeffersonians, posits Banning, had the same basic concerns about creating a government that properly balanced liberty and authority. They adapted to an American setting the ideals of that earlier generation of English Opposition writers. Believing that they were defending republicanism against the monarchistic pretensions of the Federalist party, the Jeffersonians saw their political victory in 1800 as essential to the preservation of freedom in the new nation.

Professor Banning explained his views in a lively exchange with Professor Joyce Appleby of UCLA in the January 1986 issue of *The William and Mary Quarterly*. In the essay that follows, Banning returns to one of his favorite subjects, the political creed of James Madison. He concentrates on Madison's defense of the Constitution in the Virginia ratifying convention. Observing that the Antifederalists were able men with legitimate fears of what a more vigorous national government would bring, Banning shows how Madison was pressed to make a persuasive rebuttal to their arguments. As this essay reminds us, the leaders of the Revolutionary generation—the "Founders" of popular lore—were on both sides of the debate over the Constitution.

III

1787 AND 1776: PATRICK HENRY, JAMES MADISON, THE CONSTITUTION, AND THE REVOLUTION

★

Lance Banning

[An earlier version of this essay was delivered at the Conference on First Principles of the Constitution, University of Dallas, October 17–19, 1985, and published in Sarah Baumgartner Thurow, ed., *To Secure the Blessings of Liberty: First Principles of the Constitution* (Lanham, Md.: University Press of America, 1988), 280–304.]

Scores of patriotic speakers have reminded us, of late, that the United States enjoys the oldest written constitution in the world. As we celebrate its bicentennial, however, we might also recollect the *doubts* with which the Constitution was originally received—reservations so severe and so widespread that it was barely ratified in four of thirteen states, rejected by two more. Thomas Jefferson, John Hancock, Samuel Adams, Richard Henry Lee—a formidable corps of Revolutionary heroes—all expressed significant objections. Patrick Henry thought the Constitution might betray the democratic Revolution, and Henry spoke for fully half the voters of the union's largest state, seconded by

59

several other Founding Fathers of Virginia. Only as these doubts were answered did the Constitution come to seem legitimate to many of our greatest Revolutionary statesmen; and there is much to gain from paying some attention to their fears, together with the way that they were countered. Nothing takes us more directly to the essence of the Founding vision, and perhaps no single source is more instructive on this subject than the record of debates in the Virginia ratifying convention, the only public meeting of the Revolutionary years for which we have a close approximation of a word-by-word account.[1]

From time to time, reality creates a situation and a cast no dramatist could top. It did so in the Old Dominion in 1788. Eight states had ratified the Constitution when Virginia's state convention met; nine were necessary to adopt it. No one doubted that the national decision was at stake, for all of the remaining states would follow the Virginians' lead in ratifying the reform or in insisting on conditions that were likely to defeat it.[2] Yet everyone agreed that the elections had resulted in a gathering too evenly divided to predict. Thomas Jefferson was still in France, his sentiments so mixed that Federalists and Antifederalists would both attempt to claim him. George Washington did not attend, knowing that his presence might have smacked of personal ambition while his known approval would exert a potent influence from behind the scenes. With these exceptions, though, the meeting brought together nearly every public man of major stature in the commonwealth that occupied about a fifth of the United States in 1788: James Madison, John Marshall, Edmund Pendleton, the brothers George and Wilson Cary Nicholas, George Mason, Patrick Henry, and James Monroe. Perhaps no other state—at this or any other time—could have assembled such a roll, and nowhere was the outcome so uncertain. When the meeting opened on June 3, the Federalists were marginally more optimistic than their foes, estimating a majority of three or four among the 160 present. But many delegates were wavering or undecided, and the Antifederalists believed that most of them could be persuaded to demand conditional amendments. The circumstances favored Patrick Henry, who had only to provoke more doubts than Federalists could put to rest and who was every bit as capable of dominating a Virginia public meeting as our national mythology suggests.[3]

History, regrettably, has been increasingly ungenerous to Henry, leaving most Americans with little more than foggy recollections that his speeches were supposed to mesmerize contemporary hearers. Words alone, however, barely hint at the authority with which he spoke. In 1765, when he was only twenty-nine and serving his initial term in the colonial assembly, this legendary country lawyer introduced the resolutions that ignited the colonial revolt against the Stamp Act. With Jefferson and Richard Henry Lee, he spurred Virginia's mounting protests through the next ten years and called the colony to arms in 1775 in words that countless children memorized for the centennial of American independence: "Give me liberty or give me death." First governor of his new state, an office to which he was reelected four more times within the next ten years, Henry was an aging patriot by 1788, when voters chose the special meeting that would ratify or disapprove the Constitution. Still, he gloried in his role as Revolutionary tribune of the people. And when he rose in the Convention to open the attack, referring to himself as "the servant of the people of this commonwealth, . . . a sentinel over their rights, liberty, and happiness," he summoned the assistance of a reputation only Washington's surpassed.[4]

The people, Henry said, "are exceedingly uneasy and disquieted" with this "alarming" plan "to change our government." Delegated to prepare amendments to the Articles of Confederation, the members of the Philadelphia Convention had instead proposed a change "as radical as that which separated us from Great Britain," a plan of government that would transform the United States from a Confederation into a national republic. "You ought to be extremely cautious," Henry warned. All "our privileges and rights are [once again] in danger." "A wrong step . . . now will plunge us into misery, and our republic will be lost."[5]

Language of this sort was not adopted merely for theatrical effect. When Henry spoke, the nation's republican experiment was barely twelve years old. It was by no means inconceivable that it could fail. The standard wisdom taught that a republic should be small enough and homogeneous enough that all its citizens would share a set of common interests and be able to maintain a jealous watch on the ambitions of their rulers. Now, suddenly, the Constitution offered to create a national republic larger than the largest European state. It sketched a central government whose powers would be greater than the British Parliament had claimed—a government, moreover, organized in striking imitation of the hated British form, where only the lower house of the legislature would be chosen in direct elections by the people. "I may be thought suspicious," Henry said, "but, sir, suspicion is a virtue [when] its object is the preservation of the public good."[6]

Having spent so much of his career resisting an encroaching, unresponsive central government, the aging firebrand was unmoved by Federalist insistence that rejection of the Constitution might destroy the union. He was unimpressed by Federalist descriptions of the benefits the nation could expect. Supporters of the Constitution seemed to fear, one of Henry's allies scoffed,

> that we shall have wars and rumors of wars, that every calamity is to attend us, and that we shall be ruined and disunited forever, unless we adopt this Constitution. Pennsylvania and Maryland are to fall upon us from the north, like the Goths and Vandals of old; the Algerines . . . are to fill the Chesapeake with mighty fleets, and to attack us on our front; the Indians are to invade us with numerous armies on our rear, in order to convert our cleared lands into hunting grounds; and the Carolinians, from the south, (mounted on alligators, I presume,) are to come and destroy our cornfields, and eat up our little children![7]

These were the mighty terrors, Henry sarcastically agreed, that would await Virginia if the Constitution was defeated. The nation was at peace, rapidly recovering from devastation and depression. He would not be terrified into an irreversible mistake when it was in Virginia's power to insist, at minimum, on alterations that might make the Constitution safer for the states and people.[8] Neither was he willing to concede that so much governmental power would produce the blessings some expected. "Those nations who have gone in search of grandeur, power, and splendor, have . . . been the victims of their own folly," he declaimed. "While they acquired those visionary blessings, they lost their freedom."[9] "You are not to inquire how your trade may be increased, nor how you are to become a great and powerful people, but how your liberties can be secured; for liberty ought to be the direct end of your government."[10]

Here the venerated Revolutionary loosed the whole of his impressive prowess. "Whither is the spirit of America gone?" he asked, the spirit that had checked the "pompous armaments" of mighty Britain. "It has gone," he feared,

> in search of a splendid government—a strong, energetic government. Shall we imitate the example of those nations who have gone from a simple to a splendid government? Are those nations more worthy of our imitation? What can make an adequate satisfaction to them for the loss they have suffered in attaining such a government—for the loss of their liberty? If we admit this consolidated government, it will be because we like a great, splendid one. Some way or other we must be a great and mighty empire; we must have an army, and a navy, and a number of things. When the American spirit was in its youth, the language of America was different: liberty, sir, was then the primary object.

"Consider what you are about to do," Henry pleaded. History was full of cautionary lessons, "instances of the people losing their liberty by their own carelessness and the ambition of a few." "A powerful and mighty empire," he insisted, "is incompatible with the genius of republicanism."[11]

Obviously, Henry was indulging in some verbal terrorism of his own. But this was not the language of an intellect that we can readily dismiss, and it does not suggest a thoughtless fear of extra-local power. Henry's sentiments had not been "antifederal" through most of his career, and they were antifederal now for well-considered reasons. Federalists believed that recent sectional collisions in the Continental Congress had predisposed the former governor to rail against whatever issued from the Constitutional Convention, and there can be no doubt that he opposed the Constitution partly out of a concern that vital local interests might be threatened by a stronger federal system. Nevertheless, the presence of these state and regional considerations, which were shared by Federalists and Antifederalists alike, does not suggest that either side was insincere when they addressed more theoretical concerns; and it does not permit us to conclude that this was "really" what the argument was all about.[12]

As a speaker, Patrick Henry used a shotgun, not a rapier, demolishing his target with scattershots that intermixed the trivial with the profound, sectional complaints with fundamental Revolutionary theory. But Henry's oratory lifted to inspiring heights because it rested on a base of penetrating, substantive objections. And while he often pressed the Federalists with state and regional concerns, his speeches also introduced a set of theoretical considerations that were shared by Antifederalists throughout the country, leading hundreds to conclude that this unprecedented plan of government was unacceptably at odds with the principles of 1776.[13] For the majority of people, Henry warned, national glory is a poor exchange for liberty and comfort. Whatever benefits the Constitution might appear to promise, it ought to be rejected—or at least substantially amended—if it would also prove oppressive for the body of the people. There seemed abundant reason for anticipating that it would.

When Henry warned that liberty was once again at risk, he meant, most obviously, that the new Constitution incorporated no specific guarantees of freedom of religious conscience, trial by jury, freedom of the press, or other privileges protected by the Revolutionary constitutions of the states.[14] The absence of a bill of rights was certainly the commonest and probably the most persuasive reason for opposition to the Constitution. The standard Federalist response—that it had not been necessary to deny the federal government powers it had not been granted in the first place—was entirely unconvincing, given the supremacy provision and the power to employ whatever measures might seem "necessary" to achieve enumerated ends. In Virginia, as in other states, the clamor for explicit guarantees was so widespread that Federalists were forced to promise that a bill of rights would be prepared by the new Congress once the Constitution was approved (which means, of course, that their descendants owe this fundamental charter of their freedoms, perhaps the plainest link between the Constitution and the Declaration, more to its opponents than its framers).

For many Antifederalists, however, the promise of a bill of rights was not enough. I should think that man "a lunatic," Henry exclaimed, "who should tell me to [adopt] a government avowedly defective, in hopes of having it amended afterwards." "Do you enter into a compact first, and afterwards settle the terms?"[15] Henry wanted his additional security while sovereignty still rested wholly in the people and the states, not least because addition of a bill of rights would not alleviate his deeper worries. Liberty, as every Revolutionary knew, was simply not reducible to any list of privileges on which a government would be forbidden to intrude. Liberty also meant a government directed and controlled by the body of a democratic people, which seemed, in any case, the only kind of government that would be likely to abide by written limitations on its power. This sort of liberty as well appeared to be profoundly threatened by the Constitution, which is why the fiery patriot initiated his attacks by warning that the "republic" might be lost. He did not believe that this new government would stay within the limits of its charter or, even if it did, that this would be sufficient to assure that it would prove responsive to the people's needs and will.

"This government is so new, it wants a name," Henry complained. Federalists might say that "it is national in this part, and federal in that part, &c. We may be amused, if we please, by a treatise of political anatomy," but for ordinary purposes of legislation the central government would act directly on the people, not the states.[16] It was to be a single, national government in this respect, and it would irresistibly become more national in time. Antifederalists were not persuaded by the Constitution's novel effort to divide what all the best-regarded theorists maintained could not be workably divided. Sovereignty, some Federalists had recently suggested, should not be thought of as residing in any government at all in a consistent Revolutionary order; sovereignty resided only in the people, who could certainly distribute portions of it to the states, portions to the general government, or even a concurrent jurisdiction to them both.[17] But holding to the standard view, which stated that there had to be some agency in every governmental system that would have the final power of decision, Antifederalists could not believe that neither government would really have the final say. In its attempt to balance state and federal powers, they insisted, the Constitutional Convention had created a notorious monster: an *imperium in imperio*. "I never heard of two supreme coordinate powers in one and the same country," William Grayson said. "I cannot conceive how it can happen."[18] The state and general governments, George Mason pointed out, would both possess a power of direct taxation, and they would necessarily compete for the same sources of revenue. "These two concurrent powers cannot exist long together;

the one will destroy the other; the general government being paramount to, and in every respect more powerful than the state governments, the latter must give way."[19] Sooner or later, all power would be sucked into the mighty vortex of the general government. It would be little consolation to posterity, said Henry, to know that this consolidated, unitary system had been a "mixed" one at the start.[20]

Little consolation, Henry thought, because consolidated central power would inevitably be unresponsive to the people. To many Revolutionaries this was both the clearest lesson of the colonies' rebellion against Great Britain and the irresistible conclusion of democratic logic. The size and pluralistic character of the United States were simply inconsistent with the concept of a single, national republic. George Mason, the most important framer of Virginia's state constitution, made the point in no uncertain terms. Can anyone suppose, he asked,

> that one national government will suit so extensive a country, embracing so many climates, and containing inhabitants so very different in manners, habits, and customs? . . . There never was a government over a very extensive country without destroying the liberties of the people; . . . popular government can only exist in small territories. Is there a single example, on the face of the earth, to support a contrary opinion?

"Sixty-five members," Mason reasoned, referring to the number who would sit in the first House of Representatives under the proposed Constitution, "cannot possibly know the situation and circumstances of all the inhabitants of this immense continent." But "representatives ought to . . . mix with the people, think as they think, feel as they feel,—ought to be . . . thoroughly acquainted with their interest and condition." If this were not the case, the government would not be really representative at all.[21]

Antifederalists throughout the country stressed this theme, which was nearly as ubiquitous as the demand for a bill of rights. "A full and equal representation," one of their finest writers said,

> is that which possesses the same interests, feelings, opinions, and views the people themselves would were they all assembled. A

fair representation, therefore, should be so regulated that every order of men in the community . . . can have a share in it.

And yet this federal House of Representatives would be so small that only men of great distinction could be chosen.

> If we make the proper distinction between the few men of
> wealth and abilities and consider them . . . as the natural aristoc-
> racy of the country and the great body of the people, the middle
> and lower classes, as the democracy, this federal representative
> branch will have but very little democracy in it.

With great men in the House and even greater men in the presidency and Senate, which would be chosen indirectly, all of the important powers of the nation would be lodged in "one order of men"; the many would be committed to the mercies of the few.[22]

To many Antifederalists, in short, a government was either sovereign or it was not, and genuine democracy was more than just a matter of popular elections. If the Constitution concentrated undue power in the central government (or threatened to in time), and if the powers of that government would be controlled by "representatives" unsympathetic to the needs of ordinary people, then the Constitution was profoundly flawed in its essential spirit. Insufficiently republican to start with, the structure of the general government, together with the hazy wording of its charter, would operate in practice to make it even less republican in time. First in substance, then perhaps in form as well, the system would become entirely undemocratic; the Revolution might result in nothing more than the replacement of a foreign tyranny with a domestic one. Mason had already made the point in print:

> This government will commence in a moderate aristocracy; it is
> at present impossible to foresee whether it will, in its operation,
> produce a monarchy or a corrupt, oppressive aristocracy; it will
> most probably vibrate some years between the two and then ter-
> minate in the one or the other.[23]

Grayson reinforced the argument in the Convention:

> What, sir, is the present Constitution? A republican government
> founded on the principles of . . . the British monarchy. . . . A

democratic branch marked with the strong features of aristocracy, and an aristocratic branch [the Senate] with all the impuri-
ties and imperfections of the British House of Commons, arising
from the inequality of representation and want of responsibility
[to the people].[24]

These were the features Henry had in mind when he denounced
"that paper" as "the most fatal plan that could possibly be conceived to enslave a free people."[25]

"Plan," he said, and "plan" he meant. Through all these
Antifederalist remarks there courses a profound distrust of Federalist intentions. And, indeed, in several states, the natural aristocracy was so one-sidedly in favor of the Constitution that their
uniform support confirmed the popular suspicions prompted by
the structure of the government itself. The Massachusetts state
convention, where virtually the whole elite supported ratification, elicited a memorable expression of the underlying fear:

> These lawyers, and men of learning and moneyed men, that talk
> so finely, and gloss over matters so smoothly, to make us poor
> illiterate people swallow down the pill, expect to get into Con-
> gress themselves; they expect to be managers of this Constitu-
> tion, and get all the power and all the money into their own
> hands, and then they will swallow all us little folks like the
> great *Leviathan;* yes, just as the whale swallowed up Jonah![26]

Even in Virginia, whose greatest public men were rather evenly
divided by the Constitution and usually avoided charging one
another with conspiratorial intentions, Antifederalists occasionally expressed distaste for some of the elitist phalanx who seemed
so eager for the change. Speaking as a member of the Constitutional Convention—one of three who had refused to sign—Mason
made a telling thrust:

> I have some acquaintance with a great many characters who favor
> this government, their connections, their conduct, their political
> principles. . . . There are a great many wise and good men
> among them. But when I look round . . . and observe who are
> the warmest and the most zealous friends to this new govern-
> ment, it makes me think of the story of the cat transformed into
> a fine lady; forgetting her transformation, and happening to see

a rat, she could not restrain herself, but sprang upon it out of the chair.[27]

Who would fill the powerful and lucrative positions created by the Constitution? What did its supporters really want? These were the questions Henry posed when he warned of the ambitions of the few, when he insisted that "a powerful and mighty empire is incompatible with the genius of republicanism." They were at the quick of his demand for the "real, actual, existing danger which should lead us to . . . so dangerous" a step.[28]

The challenge was in earnest, and none of these suspicions can any longer be dismissed as groundless fantasies of fearful, local politicians. Henry and his allies knew the country's situation. Most of them conceded that the powers of the central government should be enlarged. But this did not compel them to agree that there was no alternative between the unamended Constitution and anarchy or economic ruin. Neither were they wholly wrong about the motives of many advocates of constitutional reform. Since Charles Beard demythologized the making of the Constitution, twentieth-century scholarship has overwhelmingly confirmed two leading tenets of the Antifederalist position: a dispassionate consideration of the social, cultural, and economic condition of the United States during the middle 1780s does not suggest a general crisis from which it was necessary for the country to be rescued; but even cursory examination of the movement for reform *does* reveal that it derived important impetus from much of the American elite's increasing disenchantment with democracy.[29] "The Constitution," according to the leading modern student of its sources, "was intrinsically an aristocratic document designed to check the democratic tendencies of the period." Many Federalists, Gordon Wood wrote, supported the new plan of government for the same reasons that Antifederalists opposed it: because it would forbid the sort of populistic measures many states had taken in response to a severe postwar depression; because it might deliver power to a "better sort" of people; "because its very structure and detachment from the people would work to exclude . . . those who were not rich, well born, or prominent from exercising political power."[30]

Among these Federalists, moreover, were several influential individuals and groups whose discontent with democratic politics as practiced in the states was accompanied by dreams of national

grandeur very like the ones that Henry denounced. Particularly
conspicuous among the latter were the economic nationalists—
who had been seeking since early in the decade to reshape the
central government into an instrument of economic progress—
and former Continental army officers—who associated sovereignty, stability, and national prowess with a small, professional
army.[31] Rapidly emerging as a vigorous young spokesman for
these groups was Alexander Hamilton of New York, who had
spoken at the Constitutional Convention in favor of consolidated
central power and lifetime terms of office for the presidency and
Senate, who hoped to help create a thriving imperial republic,
and who did undoubtedly believe that national greatness would
require a close alliance between the country's men of liquid capi-
tal and national rulers capable of guiding and resisting the body
of the people.[32]

Mason's cat was not a phantom. Henry's dreamers of ambitious
schemes of national might and splendor were entirely real—and
likely to possess important offices if the Constitution was approved. Virginia ratified the Constitution, then, in spite of ra-
tional suspicions of the antidemocratic inclinations of many of its
friends. It ratified the Constitution in the face of deeply held and
well-considered theoretical objections to its tendencies and structure, objections capably developed by several of the state's most
honored Revolutionary heroes. How could this have happened?

Virginia ratified the Constitution, I believe, in part because
the state convention's most impressive spokesmen *for* the change
were men who did *not* share the vision Henry feared, men who
were as conscientiously concerned with Revolutionary principles
as any of their foes, men who favored the reform because they
thought it was the only way to safeguard and perfect the nation's
Revolutionary gains. To understand the Constitution's triumph
in Virginia and the nation, we need to give renewed attention to
the differences among its friends. We need to recognize that some
of these were fully as alert as Henry to the dangers he denounced
and not at all inclined to sacrifice democracy to national greatness
and prestige.

At Richmond, Henry's principal opponents were Edmund Randolph, another of the three nonsigners present at the close of the
Philadelphia Convention, and James Madison, who was more
responsible than any other individual for the distinctive shape of

constitutional reform. Randolph's stand and story, which I shall come to later, offer unexampled insight into why the Constitution was approved despite a potent fear of counterrevolution. And it is Madison, of course, to whom Americans have always turned to understand the Constitution as a Revolutionary act: the document that sealed the promises of 1776. In fact, though this has not been recognized as clearly as it should, the latter's role at Philadelphia was only the initial step in a succession of essential contributions that together justify his fame as Father of the Constitution. Hardly less important was his explanation and defense of the completed plan.[33]

Like Randolph, Madison responded to Henry's condemnation of the quest for grandeur by *agreeing* that "national splendor and glory are not our [proper] objects."[34] And when Mason said that certain clauses of the Constitution were intended to prepare the way for gradual subversion of the powers of the states, Madison immediately broke in, demanding "an unequivocal explanation" of an insinuation that all the signers of the Constitution preferred a unitary national system.[35] "If the general government were wholly independent of the governments of the particular states," he had already said, "then, indeed, usurpations might be expected to the fullest extent." But the general government, he pointed out, "derives its authority from [the state] governments and from the same sources from which their authority derives," that is, from their sovereign peoples, who would certainly resist attempted usurpations.[36] "The sum of the powers given up by the people of Virginia is divided into two classes—one to the federal and the other to the state government," Madison explained. "Each is subdivided into three branches."[37] In addition, "the powers of the federal government are enumerated; it can only operate in certain cases."[38] Far from threatening a gradual absorption of the proper powers of the people and the states, adoption of the Constitution would "increase the security of liberty more than any government that ever was," since powers ordinarily entrusted to a single government—and sometimes even to a single branch—would be distributed by the reform between two sets of governments, each of which would watch the other at the same time as its several branches served as an internal check against abuse.[39]

It is impossible to place excessive emphasis on Madison's denial that the Constitution would result in a consolidated system *or*

JAMES MADISON
Madison wanted a national government
led by virtuous men who defended
individual liberties and deferred to the
legitimate prerogatives of states.
(Courtesy of the Library of Congress)

on his disclaimer of a wish for national splendor. To him no less than to Henry, I hope to show, liberty and comfort, not riches or the might to rival European powers, were the proper tests of national happiness and greatness. And liberty, to Madison as well as his opponents, meant governments that would be genuinely responsive to the people, not merely governments that would derive from popular elections and protect the people's private rights.[40] This is why he placed such stress on the enumerated powers and complicated federal structure of the system. He did not deny that too much power, placed in hands too distant from the people, would imperil republican liberty. He even spoke occasionally of the "concessions" federal reform demanded from the people and the states.[41] He understood as well as his opponents did that national representatives would be less sympathetic to the people's local needs and better shielded from their wrath or clamors than the state assemblies. Therefore, he insisted, local interests had been left in local hands, and federal representatives would be responsible only for those great and national matters— few and carefully defined—on which they *could* be trusted to reflect the people's needs and will.[42] "As long as this is the case," he reasoned, "we have no danger to apprehend."[43]

"Where power can be *safely* lodged, if it be *necessary*," Madison maintained, "reason commands its cession."[44] It was true, of course, that every grant of power carried with it the potential for abuse, and it was true as well that Revolutionary principles demanded constant scrutiny of rulers. Yet it was also possible to carry an appropriate distrust of power to extremes that would deny the very feasibility of a republic:

> Gentlemen suppose that the general legislature will do every-thing mischievous they possibly can and that they will omit to do everything good which they are authorized to do. If this were a reasonable supposition, their objections would be good. I con-sider it reasonable to conclude that they will as readily do their duty as deviate from it; nor do I go on the grounds mentioned by gentlemen on the other side—that we are to place unlimited confidence in [national officials] and expect nothing but the most exalted integrity and sublime virtue. But I go on this great republican principle: that the people will have virtue and intelli-gence to select men of virtue and wisdom. Is there no virtue

among us? If there be not, we are in a wretched situation. No
theoretical checks, no form of government, can render us secure.
To suppose that any form of government will secure liberty or
happiness without any virtue in the people is a chimerical idea.[45]

No American has ever given deeper thought to the machinery of
government than this impressive Founder. None ever said more
clearly that mechanical contrivances are not enough. Intelligent,
attentive voters, he maintained, are necessary preconditions for a
democratic state, and the assumption that the people will repeatedly elect only those who will betray them is really an objection to
self-government itself.[46]

Apart from Mason's charge that many signers of the Constitution actually preferred a unitary system, nothing angered Madison so much as Henry's hints that only men of unsound principles
or questionable ambitions could support the proposed reform. "I
profess myself," he awkwardly exclaimed,

to have had a uniform zeal for a republican government. If the
honorable member, or any other person, conceives that my attachment to this system arises from a different source, he is mis-
taken. From the first moment that my mind was capable of con-
templating political subjects, I never, till this moment, ceased
wishing success to a well-regulated republican government.[47]

The outburst did him little credit. He ordinarily had little use for
"flaming protestations of patriotic zeal." But Madison was under-
standably infuriated by aspersions that suggested motives nearly
opposite to those he felt. For he not only thought the Constitution
perfectly consistent with republican philosophy, but he questioned
whether there was any other means by which the Revolution could
be saved.

Henry challenged his opponents to explain the "actual, existing danger" that compelled so great a change. No one, then or
later, could explain it more completely than this modest little
Framer. The history of the Confederation, Madison insisted, offered "repeated unequivocal proofs . . . of the utter inutility and
inefficacy" of a central government that depended on thirteen
other governments for revenues and for enforcement of its laws,
proofs confirmed by the experiences of other historical confedera-

cies.[48] "The Confederation is so notoriously feeble," he continued, "that foreign nations are unwilling to form any treaties with us," for these had been "violated at pleasure by the states." Congress was "obliged to borrow money even to pay the interest of our debts," although these debts had been incurred in the sacred cause of independence.[49] It was evident, accordingly, when delegates assembled for the Constitutional Convention, that the nation could no longer trust its "happiness" and "safety" to "a government totally destitute of the means of protecting itself or its members."[50] And Revolutionary principles themselves required that independent taxing powers and independent means of compelling obedience to federal laws should rest directly on the people, not the states.[51]

But national humiliation and dishonor, disgraceful though these were, were only part of the impending peril as Madison perceived it. Members of a union were entitled to expect the general government to defend their happiness and safety, which were gravely damaged by the economic dislocations caused by British restrictions on American commerce. Nonetheless, the Continental Congress had been checked in every effort to secure a power to retaliate against the British, and states attempting independent actions had been checked by the competing laws of neighbors.[52] Discontent with the Confederation and hostility between the states had led to open talk of the replacement of the general union by several smaller confederacies, and Madison did not believe that the republican experiment could long outlive the continental union. At the Philadelphia Convention he had said:

> Let each state depend on itself for its security, and let apprehensions arise of danger from distant powers or from neighboring states, and the languishing condition of all the states, large as well as small, would soon be transformed into vigorous and high toned governments. . . . The same causes which have rendered the old world the theatre of incessant wars and have banished liberty from the face of it, would soon produce the same effects here. [The smaller states would] quickly introduce some regular military force against sudden danger from their powerful neighbors. The example . . . would soon become universal. [Great powers would be granted to executives.] A standing military force, with an overgrown executive, will not long be safe companions to liberty.[53]

Writing in *The Federalist,* he had again affirmed the warning. "Nothing short of a Constitution fully adequate to the national defense and the preservation of the Union can save America from as many standing armies" as there are states or separate confederacies, he insisted, "and from such a progressive augmentation of these establishments in each as will render them . . . burdensome to the properties and ominous to the liberties of the people." Without the general union, liberty would everywhere be "crushed between standing armies and perpetual taxes."[54] The Revolutionary order would collapse.

Henry "tells us the affairs of our country are not alarming," Madison complained. "I wish this assertion was well founded."[55] In fact, the Constitutional Convention had assembled in the midst of an immediate crisis of American union, and the union was the necessary shield for the republican experiment that Henry wanted to preserve. Nor was even this the sum of current dangers. The Convention also faced a second crisis, which Henry failed to recognize in his repeated condemnations of "the tyranny of rulers." In republics, Madison suggested, "turbulence, violence, and abuse of power by the majority trampling on the rights of the minority . . . have, more frequently than any other cause, produced despotism." In the United States—and even in Virginia— it was not the acts of unresponsive rulers, but the follies and transgressions of the sympathetic representatives of state majorities that tempted growing numbers of the people to abandon their Revolutionary convictions. "The only possible remedy for those evils," he protested, the only one consistent with "preserving and protecting the principles of republicanism, will be found in that very system which is now exclaimed against as the parent of oppression."[56]

With these words the Framer introduced the train of reasoning that had produced another of his crucial contributions to the Founding. In every state the popular assemblies had struggled to protect their citizens from the economic difficulties of the middle 1780s. Many of their measures—paper money, laws suspending private suits for debt, postponements of taxation, or continued confiscations of the property of former Loyalists—had interfered with private contracts, endangered people's right to hold their property secure, or robbed the states of the resources necessary to fulfill their individual and federal obligations. Essentially unchecked by other parts of government, the lower houses had ignored state bills of rights and sacrificed the long-term interests of the whole community to more immediate considerations, calling into question, Madison had said, "the fundamental principle of republican government, that the majority who rule in such governments are the safest guardians both of public good and of private rights."[57]

Although Virginia managed to avoid the worst abuses of the middle eighties, Madison thought continentally. As the country moved toward constitutional reform, correspondents had alerted him to growing disillusionment with popular misgovernment—particularly in New England, where Shays's Rebellion erupted in the winter of 1786. Virginia's own immunity from popular commotions or majority misrule appeared to him in doubt. Personally revolted by the changeability, injustices, and lack of foresight of even Virginia's laws, he did not abandon his republican commitment; but he did become increasingly concerned that disenchantment with democracy, confined thus far to only a tiny (though an influential) few, could spread in time through growing numbers of the people, who might eventually prefer a despotism or hereditary rule to governments unable to secure their happiness or even to protect their fundamental rights.[58] The crisis of Confederation government, as Madison conceived it, was compounded by a crisis of republican convictions, and the interlocking dangers could be overcome only by a change that would at once "perpetuate the union and redeem the honor of the republican name."[59] He therefore went to Philadelphia to urge abandonment of the Confederation in favor of a carefully constructed great republic, which would rise directly from the people, could be trusted with effective, full, and independent powers over matters of general concern, and would incorporate so many different economic interests and religious sects that majorities would seldom form "on any other principles than those of justice and the general good."[60] Although the full Convention greatly modified his own proposals, he soon concluded that the finished Constitution was the best—and possibly the final—opportunity to reconcile democracy with private rights and public good. He even came to reason that the complicated, federal features of the finished Constitution would provide additional securities that he had not envisioned when the great Convention met.

Madison assumed a very special place among the Founders—more special, I would argue, even than is commonly believed—because he personally bridged so much of the abyss between the Revolutionary tribunes such as Henry and the aspiring consuls such as Hamilton, with whom he formed a brief and less-than-wholly-comfortable alliance. He fully shared with higher-flying Federalists not only the determination to invigorate the union, but also the emotional rejection of the early Revolutionary constitutions and the populistic politics that they permitted—what Elbridge Gerry called "an excess of democracy."[61] He believed, as Hamilton believed, that Revolutionary governments were so responsive to the wishes of unhampered, temporary state majorities that they endangered the unalienable rights that independence was intended to protect. He agreed with other Federalists that just, enduring governments demanded qualities not found in popular assemblies: protection for the propertied minority (and others); the wisdom to discern the long-term general good; and power to defend them both against more partial, more immediate considerations.

No more than Henry, though, did Madison approve the vision of a splendid, mighty future; and whatever was the case with other Federalists, his fear of the majority was always fully counterbalanced by continuing awareness of the dangers posed by unresponsive rulers or excessive central power. Hamilton and other economic nationalists hoped to use a stronger central government to speed developments that would prepare the groundwork for successful competition with the great Atlantic empires. Madison intended to "perpetuate the union" in order to *preserve* the Revolution from the European curses of professional armed forces, persistent public debts, powerful executives, and swollen taxes, as well as to invest the general government with the ability to counteract the European trading policies that seemed to him to threaten the social foundations of American democracy.[62] Some members of the Constitutional Convention may have wanted to create a system that would place as much authority as possible in rulers only distantly dependent on the people. But Madison expected to create a government that would defeat the wishes of factional majorities *without* destroying the republican "communion of interests and sympathy of sentiments" between the rulers and the ruled.[63] Although he shared the hope that large election districts would result in representatives who would resist unjust majority demands, he had been equally concerned, throughout the Constitutional Convention, to control potentially ambitious rulers and assure that they could never free themselves from their dependence on the people.[64] In *The Federalist* and in Virginia's state convention, the Constitution he defended *would* "break and control the violence" of factions and assure superior attention to the long-term good,[65] but it would *not* produce a government that would be unresponsive to the people's needs or will. Responsibility would be secured, as always, by popular elections and internal checks and balances. For the first time in the history of representative democracy, it would be further guaranteed by the enumerated limits and the compound, federal features of the reconstructed system.

Recent scholarship has not placed equal emphasis on all the vital parts of Madison's attempt to understand and justify the Constitution. It credits him, of course, with an essential role in the creation of a central government whose parts would all derive from popular elections, as well as with the most elaborate defense of its republican characteristics. It devotes elaborate attention to his argument that private rights are safer in a large than in a small republic. It leans on him, indeed—more heavily than it relies on any other individual—for its recognition that "the Constitution presented no simple choice between accepting or rejecting the principles of 1776," since the Federalists could "intelligibly picture themselves as the true defenders of the libertarian tradition."[66] In doing so, however, it commonly identifies the man too closely with the movement, makes too much of some ideas and not enough of others, and thus obscures some differences that had important consequences in Virginia and the country as a whole.

"There is something decidedly disingenuous," writes Gordon Wood, "about the democratic radicalism" of Federalist defenses of the Constitution, for behind this language lay an evident desire "for a high-toned government filled with better sorts of people, . . . partisan and aristocratic purposes that belied the Federalists' democratic language."[67] For many Federalists, no doubt, this characterization is quite apt; and yet a careful effort to distinguish Madison's position from that of other key reformers—one that gives full weight to his insistence on the complicated federal structure and enumerated powers of the central government, his fear of independent rulers, and his conviction that the Constitution was a wholly democratic remedy for democratic ills—both qualifies and clarifies Wood's generalization. The Federalists did generally believe that private rights and public happiness were threatened in the states by populistic politics and poorly balanced constitutions. They looked to federal reform not only as a necessary cure for the debilities of the Confederation, but also as an opportunity to remedy those other ills; and they believed a proper remedy required both limitations on the states and the erection of a general government that would be more resistant to majority demands. Madison not only shared these wishes but he was more responsible than any other thinker for defining problems in these terms and sketching leading features of the Federalist solution. But this was only part—and not the most distinctive part—of Madison's peculiar contribution.

What distinguished Madison most clearly from all the other Framers was his early, firm, and intimate association of survival of the union with continuation of a Revolutionary enterprise he still defined, in insufficiently acknowledged ways, in early Revolutionary terms. The liberty he wished to save—the point requires repeated stress—was not just liberty defined as the inherent rights of individuals, but also liberty defined as popular self-governance.[68] Convinced that neither sort of liberty could be secure without the other, valuing them both, he worked from the beginning for a change that would restrain tyrannical majorities; and yet he never doubted that majorities should rule—or that the people *would* control the complicated structure raised by the completed Constitution. This is why he heatedly denied that he approved of a consolidated system, placed increasing emphasis on federal dimensions of the structure, and properly insisted that he had no other object than the people's liberty and comfort. He was defending a reform that he had always understood—and was still trying to define—as an attempt to rescue *both* of the ideals enunciated in the Declaration: private rights, but also popular self-rule.[69]

To fully understand his vital part in the creation of the federal republic, it is critical to see that Madison's determination to achieve a change that would secure both private rights *and* public liberty extended far beyond adjournment of the Constitutional Convention, that his effort to legitimize the Constitution from the vantage point of Revolutionary theory was nearly as important to its triumph as his contributions to its framing. Edmund Randolph's story illustrates these points, as does the rest of Madison's career.

A close associate of Madison since 1776 and governor of Virginia when the Constitutional Convention met, Randolph introduced the plan with which the Philadelphia deliberations started. Like Mason, he contributed effectively to the Convention's work but grew increasingly alarmed as the proceedings altered Madison's original proposals. Sharing Mason's doubts about a strong, reeligible executive, a Senate dominated by the smaller, northern states, the hazy wording of important clauses, and the motives of some of his colleagues, Randolph was the first of three nonsigners to declare that he could not approve the finished Constitution, hoping for the meeting of a second general convention to repair the oversights and errors of the first. Nonetheless, when the Virginia state convention met, he startled the assemblage by immediately announcing that, despite his reservations, he would unequivocally support the unamended Constitution. He took the lead, in fact, from the beginning, as a fervent foe of a conditional approval of the plan.[70]

What had happened in the intervening months to change his mind? Henry pressed him with this question to the point of personal exchanges that provided the dramatic highlight of the meeting.[71] The response was fundamentally uncomplicated but revealing. "I refused to sign," Randolph answered, "because I had, as I still have, objections to the Constitution, and wished a free inquiry into its merits." At that time, it had still seemed possible to work for previous amendments. Now, however, eight of thirteen states had ratified the unamended Constitution. In these different circumstances, to insist on previous amendments was impossible "without inevitable ruin to the Union, and . . . I will assent to the lopping of this limb [meaning his arm] before I assent to the dissolution of the Union."[72] The old Confederation, Randolph said, "is gone, whether this house says so or not. It is gone, sir, by its own weakness."[73] The eight approving states would not recede to gratify Virginia. To insist on previous amendments now could only prove "another name for rejection." "If, in this situation, we reject the Constitution, the Union will be dissolved, the dogs of war will break loose, and anarchy and discord will complete the ruin of this country."[74]

Henry feared the Revolution would be lost. "I am a child of the Revolution," Randolph replied. "I would join heart and hand in rejecting the system did I not conceive it would promote our happiness." But the Constitution offered new securities against "injustice, licentiousness, insecurity, and oppression,"[75] and Virginia could not "exist without a union with her neighbors"—not, at least, as a republic.

> Those states, . . . our friends, brothers, and supporters, will, if disunited from us, be our bitterest enemies. . . . The other states have upwards of 330,000 men capable of bearing arms. . . . In case of an attack, what defense can we make? . . . Our export trade is entirely in the hands of foreigners. We have no manufactures. . . . Shall we form a partial confederacy? . . . Partial confederacies will require such a degree of force and expense as will destroy every feature of republicanism.[76]

"Is this government necessary for the safety of Virginia?" Randolph asked. For him, it was the final question, and he answered it as Madison had answered it nine months before. "Could I . . . believe that there . . . was no storm gathering," that previous amendments could really be secured, "I would concur" with Henry's plan, "for nothing but the fear of inevitable destruction would lead me to vote for the Constitution in spite of the objections I have."[77] But the approval of eight states, the governor repeated, had reduced the issue "to the single question of Union or no Union."[78] And among Virginia's vital interests, Randolph thought, none was dearer than the state's survival as a liberal republic. "When I see safety on my right, and destruction on my left, . . . I cannot hesitate to decide in favor of the former."[79]

How many moderates (or "trimmers" in contemporary parlance) reasoned much as Randolph did? It is impossible to know—and certainly impossible to say, as we can say with certainty in Randolph's case, how many were directly influenced by James Madison.[80] It is a fact, however, that in all the narrowly divided states, the ratification contest was decided in the end by a handful of uncertain, silent delegates who, at the final moment, proved unwilling to insist on previous amendments at the risk of dissolution of the union. It is not unreasonable to guess that, like the two Virginians, many of them thought that democratic liberty could only thrive within the federal hedge. Many of them may have hoped, as Madison and Randolph hoped, that private rights and public liberty would both prove more secure in an enlarged, compound republic. Madison was not, of course, the only Federalist to reason in these terms, but he was undeniably the earliest and most effective spokesman for a train of thought on which, among a Revolutionary generation, the triumph of the Constitution may have turned.[81]

The victory was narrow, to be sure, and incomplete. A motion to insist on previous amendments was defeated eighty-eight to eighty. Virginia ratified the Constitution by a margin of ten votes and recommended numerous amendments to the first new Congress.[82] Though Madison had plausibly defended every clause—and Washington, as everyone had hoped, was the unanimous selection of the first electoral college—many children of the Revolution entered on the federal experiment with all the reservations Randolph swallowed. A few proclaimed, as Patrick Henry did, that they would work with all their power "to retrieve the loss of liberty, and remove the defects of that system in a constitutional way."[83] Madison himself, however, was far from finished with his effort to define a genuinely Revolutionary, partly national, but also partly federal union. The skeptics therefore found a potent, partial ally in the Father of the Constitution, who quickly joined with Thomas Jefferson to lead most of the former Antifederalists into a party dedicated to a strict interpretation of the federal charter and a vision of the future much at odds with Hamilton's design for national glory. That Madison would take this stand should not seem so surprising as many analysts have thought.

Notes

1. We owe the record to an enterprising shorthand reporter, David Robertson, who published the proceedings later in the year. They are conveniently reprinted in Jonathan Elliot, ed., *The Debates in the Several State Conventions on the Adoption of the Federal Constitution,* 2d ed., 5 vols. (Philadelphia: J. B. Lippincott, 1901), vol. 3 [hereafter referred to as Elliot, *Debates*). A recent article has warned that we cannot depend on Robertson's reporting with the same degree of confidence that could be placed in a modern, stenographic record, but I see little reason to believe that it is not essentially dependable for the purposes of this essay. See James H. Hutson, "The Creation of the Constitution: The Integrity of the Documentary Record," *Texas Law Review* 65 (1986): 23–24.

2. Although the news did not reach Richmond in time to influence the decision, New Hampshire ratified the Constitution on June 21, four days before Virginia. Historians agree that its approval may have made slight difference. If Virginia, North Carolina, and New York had nonetheless held out, it seems unlikely that the document could actually have gone into effect.

3. For initial estimates by leaders on both sides, see Madison to Washington, June 4, 1788, Robert A. Rutland et al., eds., *The Papers of James Madison,* 14 vols. (Chicago: University of Chicago Press, 1975), 10:400; Robert A. Rutland, ed., *The Papers of George Mason, 1725–1792,* 3 vols. (Chapel Hill: University of North Carolina Press, 1970), 3:1040, 1044–46; and William Wirt Henry, *Patrick Henry: Life, Correspondence, and Speeches,* 3 vols., rev. ed. (New York: Burt Franklin, 1969), 2:342–43. As everywhere, though there were numerous exceptions, the least commercial portions of the state (the Southside) tended to oppose the Constitution, the most commercial portions (e.g., the Northern Neck) tended to approve it, and the central Piedmont was divided. For the nature and closeness of the popular division, see Norman K. Risjord, *Chesapeake Politics, 1781–1800* (New York: Columbia University Press, 1978), 293–317; Risjord, "Virginians and the Constitution: A Multivariant Analysis," *William and Mary Quarterly* 31 (1974): 3:613–32; Norman K. Risjord and Gordon DenBoer, "The Evolution of Political Parties in Virginia, 1782–1800," *Journal of American History* 60 (1974): 961–84; Robert E. Thomas, "The Virginia Convention of 1788: A Criticism of Beard's *An Economic Interpretation of the Constitution,*" *Journal of Southern History* 19 (1953): 63–72; Jackson Turner Main, *Political Parties before the Constitution* (Chapel Hill: University of North Carolina Press, 1973); and Forrest McDonald, *We The People: The Economic Origins of the Constitution* (Chicago: University of Chicago Press, 1958). The best short narratives of the Convention include Gordon DenBoer, "The House of Delegates and the Evolution of Political Parties in Virginia, 1782–1792" (Ph.D. diss., University of Wisconsin, 1972), chap. 6; David John Mays, *Edmund Pendleton, 1721–1803: A Biography,* 2 vols. (Cambridge, Mass.: Harvard University Press, 1952), 2:217–72; and Jackson Turner Main,

The Antifederalists: Critics of the Constitution, 1781–1788 (Chapel Hill: University of North Carolina Press, 1961), 223–33. The fullest is still Hugh Blair Grigsby, *History of the Virginia Federal Convention of 1788*, 2 vols. (Virginia Historical Society, *Collections*, 2:9–10 [Richmond, 1890–91]).

4. Robert Douthat Meade, *Patrick Henry*, 2 vols. (Philadelphia, 1957–69); Richard R. Beeman, *Patrick Henry: A Biography* (New York: McGraw-Hill, 1974). The quotation is from Elliot, *Debates*, 3:21.

5. This summarizes parts of Henry's first two speeches in the Convention, from Elliot, *Debates*, 3:21–23, 44–45. Throughout the essay I have expanded abbreviations, corrected slips of the pen, and slightly modernized the punctuation and capitalization wherever this appeared to make a passage easier for twentieth-century readers.

6. Ibid., 45.

7. William Grayson, ibid., 277.

8. Ibid., 62–63.

9. Ibid., 47.

10. Ibid., 44–45.

11. Ibid., 46, 48, 53–54.

12. I have examined the Convention from this alternative perspective in "Virginia: Nation, State, and Section," a paper delivered at the conference on "Ratifying the Constitution: Ideas and Interests in the Several American States," National Humanities Center, May 21–24, 1987, in Michael Lienesch and Michael Gillispie, eds., *Ratifying the Constitution: Ideas and Interests in the Several American States* (Lawrence, Kans.: University Press of Kansas, 1988), forthcoming.

13. Antifederalist writings have recently been collected in Herbert J. Storing, ed., *The Complete Anti-Federalist*, 7 vols. (Chicago: University of Chicago Press, 1981). The most important secondary studies are the general introduction to Storing's collection, available separately as *What the Anti-Federalists Were For: The Political Thought of the Opponents of the Constitution* (Chicago: University of Chicago Press, 1981); Main, *Antifederalists;* and the introduction to Cecelia M. Kenyon, ed., *The Antifederalists* (Indianapolis: Bobbs-Merrill, 1966). For additional recent writings see James H. Hutson, "Country, Court, and Constitution: Antifederalism and the Historians," *William and Mary Quarterly* 38 (1981): 3:337–68.

14. Elliot, *Debates*, 3:44.

15. Ibid., 176, 591.

16. Ibid., 160, 171.

17. The fullest discussion of Revolutionary changes in the concept of sovereignty is in Gordon S. Wood, *The Creation of the American Republic, 1776–1787* (Chapel Hill: University of North Carolina Press, 1969). See also Gordon S. Wood, "The Political Ideology of the Founders," in this volume.

18. Elliot, *Debates*, 3:281.

19. Ibid., 29–30.

20. Ibid., 171.

21. Ibid., 30, 32. For Mason see, Robert A. Rutland, *George Mason: Reluctant Statesman* (Williamsburg, Va.: Colonial Williamsburg, 1961), and Helen Hill Miller, *George Mason: Gentleman Revolutionary* (Chapel Hill: University of North Carolina Press, 1975).

22. Walter Hartwell Bennett, ed., *Letters from the Federal Farmer to the Republican* (University: University of Alabama Press, 1978), 10, 14, 22. See also, more largely, 47–52.

Bennett writes that the evidence for the traditional attribution of these letters to Richard Henry Lee, "while strong, hardly seems sufficient to justify continuing this attribution" (20). The attribution was disputed to my satisfaction in Gordon S. Wood, "The Authorship of the *Letters from the Federal Farmer,*" *William and Mary Quarterly* 31 (1974): 3:299–308. A plausible but not compelling alternative attribution has recently been suggested in Robert H. Webking, "Melancton Smith and the *Letters from the Federal Farmer,*" *William and Mary Quarterly* 44 (1987): 510–28.

23. "Objections to the Proposed Federal Constitution," in Kenyon, *Antifederalists,* 195.

24. Elliot, *Debates,* 3:280.

25. Ibid., 176.

26. Amos Singletary, ibid., 2:102.

27. Ibid., 3:269.

28. Ibid., 23.

29. The landmark studies were Charles A. Beard, *An Economic Interpretation of the Constitution of the United States* (New York: Macmillan, 1913); Merrill Jensen, *The Articles of Confederation: An Interpretation of the Social-Constitutional History of the American Revolution, 1774–1781* (Madison: University of Wisconsin Press, 1940); and Jensen, *The New Nation: A History of the United States during the Confederation, 1781–1789* (New York: Vintage Books, 1950).

30. Wood, *Creation of the American Republic,* 513–14.

31. See especially E. James Ferguson, *The Power of the Purse: A History of American Public Finance, 1776–1790* (Chapel Hill: University of North Carolina Press, 1961); Ferguson, "The Nationalists of 1781–1783 and the Economic Interpretation of the Constitution," *Journal of American History* 56 (1969): 241–61; and Richard H. Kohn, *Eagle and Sword: The Federalists and the Creation of the Military Establishment in America, 1783–1802* (New York: Free Press, 1975).

32. Biographies include John C. Miller, *Alexander Hamilton: Portrait in Paradox* (New York: Macmillan, 1959); Forrest McDonald, *Alexander Hamilton: A Biography* (New York: Norton, 1979); and Jacob Ernest Cooke, *Alexander Hamilton* (New York: Norton, 1982). See also Gerald Stourzh, *Alexander Hamilton and the Idea of Republican Government* (Stanford, Calif.: Stanford University Press, 1970).

33. For biographical information see Irving Brant, *James Madison,* 6 vols. (Indianapolis: Bobbs-Merrill, 1941–61); Ralph Ketcham, *James Madison: A Biography* (New York: Macmillan, 1971); and Harold S. Schultz, *James Madison* (New York: Twayne, 1970).

34. Elliot, *Debates,* 3:135. For Randolph, see ibid., 81.

35. Mason insisted that many members of the Convention *had* desired consolidation, but that Madison had "expressed himself against it" in a private conversation and that he had never heard any Virginia delegate advocate a unitary system. Madison "declared himself satisfied," and Mason finished his speech (ibid., 517–30). Hugh Blair Grigsby, whose *History of the Virginia Federal Convention of 1788* was based in part on oral information, was being overly dramatic when he wrote that Madison "demanded reparation in a tone that menaced an immediate call to the field" (90), but there can be no doubt that the Framer sharply resented the remark. Madison was universally described as a man of remarkably "sweet" manners, who never lost his temper; but he was capable of flashes of hard anger—and an uncharacteristic breach of parliamentary decorum—when he thought himself accused of consolidationism or when someone seemed to doubt his commitment to republicanism.

36. Elliot, *Debates,* 3:96.

37. Ibid., 408–9.

38. Ibid., 95.

39. Ibid., 408–9. Madison's most elaborate explanations of the partly federal, partly national derivation and structure of the new system—and of the guarantees against a further consolidation—include his speeches of June 6 and 11, pp. 94–97, 257–59, and especially *Federalist* Nos. 39, 45, 46, 51, and 62.

40. "The genius of republican liberty" demands "not only that all power should be derived from the people, but that those entrusted with it should be kept in dependence on the people." *Federalist* 37:227.

41. To Thomas Jefferson, March 19, 1787, see Rutland et al., *Papers of James Madison*, 9:318. See also his reference in the state convention in Elliot, *Debates*, 3:95, to the necessity of "submitting to the inconvenience" of greater federal power.

42. *Federalist* 10:82–83. But there are any number of indications that Madison assumed that federal representatives would reflect their constituents' will, which was a logical necessity for his argument that the large republic would defeat factious majorities. Among the clearest are *Federalist* 46:296–97, 51:325, and especially 57:350–53.

43. Elliot, *Debates*, 3:90.

44. Ibid., 394 (*emphasis* added).

45. Ibid., 536–37.

46. *Federalist* 57:350–53.

47. Elliot, *Debates*, 3:394.

48. Ibid., 128–29ff. For the experiences of other confederacies, see *Federalist* Nos. 18–20.

49. Elliot, *Debates*, 3:135–36. On the debts, see his eloquent "Address to the States" of April 26, 1783, in Rutland et al., *Papers of James Madison*, 6:494: "The citizens of the U.S. are responsible for the greatest trust ever confided to a political society. If justice, good faith, honor, gratitude, and all the other qualities which ennoble the character of a nation and fulfill the ends of government be the fruits of our [republican] establishments, the cause of liberty will acquire a dignity and lustre which it has never yet enjoyed; and an example will be set which cannot but have the most favorable influence on the rights of mankind. If, on the other side, our governments should be unfortunately blotted with the reverse of these cardinal and essential virtues, the great cause which we have engaged to vindicate will be dishonored and betrayed; the last and fairest experiment in favor of the rights of human nature will be turned against them; and their patrons and friends exposed to be insulted and silenced by the votaries of tyranny and usurpation."

50. Elliot, *Debates*, 3:129.

51. Madison's earliest sketch of a reform (to Jefferson, March 19, 1787, Rutland et al., *Papers of James Madison*, 9:318–19) suggested that an independent federal taxing power would require a reconstitution of Congress on the basis of proportional representation. Jefferson approved the power and likewise insisted that the reform must "preserve inviolate the fundamental principle that the people are not to be taxed but by representatives chosen immediately by themselves" (10:336).

52. This was clearly the problem that first led Madison to approve a thorough reconsideration of the structure of the Confederation. For elaboration and citations see Lance Banning, "James Madison and the Nationalists, 1780–1783," *William and Mary Quarterly* 40 (1983): 3:252–53.

53. Speech of June 29 in Max Farrand, ed., *The Records of the Federal Convention of 1787*,

rev. ed., 4 vols. (New Haven, Conn.: Yale University Press, 1966), 1:464–65 [hereafter referred to as Farrand, *Records*].

54. *Federalist* 41:259–60, and passim. See also Elliot, *Debates,* 3:382.

55. Elliot, *Debates,* 3:399.

56. Ibid., 87–88. And see, of course, the famous, earlier elaborations of the point in *Federalist* Nos. 10 and 51: "The instability, injustice, and confusion introduced into the public councils have, in truth, been the mortal diseases under which popular governments have everywhere perished. . . . Complaints are everywhere heard from our most considerate and virtuous citizens, equally the friends of public and private faith and of public and personal liberty, that our governments are too unstable, that the public good is disregarded in the conflicts of rival parties, and that measures are too often decided, not according to the rules of justice and the rights of the minor party, but by the superior force of an interested and overbearing majority" (10:77). "Justice is the end of government. It is the end of civil society. It ever has been and ever will be pursued until it be obtained, or until liberty be lost in the pursuit" (51:324).

57. "Vices of the Political System of the United States," April, 1787, in Rutland et al., *Papers of James Madison,* 10:354. See also "Observations on Jefferson's Draft of a Constitution for Virginia," ibid., 11:287–88. It should be noted, though, that Madison did not consider the "mutability" of laws to be pernicious to minorities alone. "Instability," says Madison in *Federalist* 62, gives an "unreasonable advantage . . . to the sagacious, the enterprising, and the moneyed few over the industrious and uninformed mass of the people. Every new regulation concerning commerce or revenue, or in any manner affecting the value of the different species of property, presents a new harvest to those who watch the change. . . . But the most deplorable effect of all is that diminution of attachment and reverence which steals into the hearts of the people towards a political system which betrays so many marks of infirmity, and disappoints so many . . . hopes" (381, 382).

58. Madison's letters to Virginia from his seat in the Confederation Congress during February and March 1787 reported widespread suspicions of a growth of pro-monarchy sentiments in New England. See, for example, the letter to Washington of February 21, Rutland et al., *Papers of James Madison,* 9:286. His fear of this phenomenon was very near the surface when he outlined his earliest ideas about reform in the letter to Jefferson of March 19 (ibid., 318), writing that "the mortal diseases of the existing constitution . . . have tainted the faith of the most orthodox republicans, and . . . challenge from the votaries of liberty every concession in favor of stable government not infringing fundamental principles as the only security against an opposite extreme of our present situation."

59. To Edmund Pendleton, February 24, 1787, in ibid., 295.

60. *Federalist* 51:325.

61. Farrand, *Records,* 1:48.

62. On the last point see Drew R. McCoy, *The Elusive Republic: Political Economy in Jeffersonian America* (Chapel Hill: University of North Carolina Press, 1980).

63. *Federalist* 57:352. This number is Madison's most complete explanation of the forces that would keep federal representatives responsive to the people.

64. Ibid., 51:321–22. For a reinterpretation of Madison's course at the Convention, see Lance Banning, "The Practicable Sphere of a Republic: James Madison, the Constitutional Convention, and the Emergence of Revolutionary Federalism," in Richard Beeman et al., eds., *Beyond Confederation: Origins of the Constitution and American National Identity* (Chapel Hill: University of North Carolina Press, 1987), 162–87.

65. *Federalist* 10:77.

66. Wood, *Creation of the American Republic,* 523–24.

67. Ibid., 562, 615.

68. *Federalist* 39:240: Only a "strictly republican" form of government "would be reconcilable with the genius of the people of America; with the fundamental principles of the revolution; or with that honorable determination which animates every votary of freedom to rest all our political experiments on the capacity of mankind for self-government."

69. I have developed many of these points at greater length in "James Madison and the Nationalists"; "The Practicable Sphere of a Republic"; and "The Hamiltonian Madison: A Reconsideration," *Virginia Magazine of History and Biography* 92 (1984): 3–28.

70. A modern biography is John J. Reardon, *Edmund Randolph: A Biography* (New York: Macmillan, 1974).

71. See especially Elliot, *Debates,* 3:187–89. Grigsby, in *History of the Virginia Federal Convention of 1788,* 165, says that in the evening after this exchange Colonel William Cabell called on Randolph as a friend of Henry, but that the Convention was relieved to learn the next morning that a reconciliation had been achieved without a recourse to the field. I doubt that there was any serious consideration of a duel, but Randolph *had* used language that one gentleman did not use to another.

72. Elliot, *Debates,* 3:24–26, 652.

73. Ibid., 84.

74. Ibid., 603.

75. Ibid., 65, 67.

76. Ibid., 72–80.

77. Ibid., 596–97.

78. Ibid., 652.

79. Ibid., 66.

80. Madison's successful effort in the months between the two conventions to persuade his friend to cooperate with the Federalists on the Massachusetts plan of recommendatory amendments can be followed in full in volumes 10–11 of Rutland et al., *Papers of James Madison.*

81. In addition to the sources cited in notes 52–54 above, see Madison's insistence, at Philadelphia as well as Richmond, that the South would be especially vulnerable in the event of a collapse of the union in Farrand, *Records,* 2:306–7, 361, 451–52; Elliot, *Debates,* 3:251, 621.

82. The recommended amendments, a bill of rights and several substantive changes in the powers and structure of the new government, are in Elliot, *Debates,* 3:657–61. The outcome would suggest (see note 3 above) that the Federalists debated their opponents to, at worst, a draw. They probably maintained and may have slightly widened the narrow margin with which they began.

83. Ibid., 652.

A s Gordon Wood and Lance Banning have noted in their essays, the Founders were concerned with the promotion of "virtue" in the new nation. In the next essay, written after the BYU lecture series ended, Richard Vetterli and Gary Bryner contend that religious ideas played a large part in shaping the American understanding of virtue. They hereby summarize arguments first made in their recently published *In Search of the Republic* (Totowa, N.J.: Rowman and Littlefield, 1987).

Vetterli and Bryner are natives of Salt Lake City, Utah. Vetterli received his Ph.D. in political science from the University of California, Riverside (1962) after earning his M.A. at UCLA and B.A. from Brigham Young University. He has taught at Pepperdine University, Pasadena City College, and is currently a professor of political science at Brigham Young University. Bryner attended the University of Utah, where he took a B.A. in economics; he went on for a Ph.D. in political science at Cornell University (1982). He came from the Brookings Institution to Brigham Young University in 1982, where he is now an associate professor of political science.

Professors Vetterli and Bryner emphasize the importance of the Constitution in the national quest for a return to "first principles." Their view should be contrasted with that of John Diggins, whose essay follows. Thus, while these authors agree in part on the source of American ideas about virtue, they have different perspectives on how significant a role virtue played in the founding of the republic. That they disagree on some issues even as they agree on others should serve as a reminder that disputes about the Constitution did not end with the original Federalist–Antifederalist debate. Perhaps our willingness to reexamine and reevaluate the Constitution is a sign of our political vitality, just as reluctance to do so could indicate growing malaise.

IV

RELIGION, PUBLIC VIRTUE, AND THE FOUNDING OF THE AMERICAN REPUBLIC

★

Richard Vetterli

Gary C. Bryner

Public virtue was central to the political system envisioned by the Framers of the Constitution. Public spiritedness, a willingness to pursue the common good, self-restraint in the pursuit of self-interest, benevolence, and charity, they believed, were essential for the practice of republican government and politics. Public virtue was at the foundation of representative government because voters were expected to select leaders who, in James Madison's words, "possess most wisdom to discern, and most virtue to pursue, the common good of the society."[1]

How was public virtue to be assured? The Framers rejected the classical idea that the state was responsible for the inculcation of virtue. The common good and the interests of others—not enhancing the power of the state—were the goals of public life. The "genius" of the American people that made self-government possible was rooted in their political culture, in a popular commitment to social peace and harmony, and in a fusion of personal and public virtue. The structure of government—the separation of powers and checks and balances—were "auxiliary precautions" against the excesses of governmental power; "a dependence on the people," argued Madison, "is, no doubt, the primary control on the government."[2] The Framers never abandoned the idea of public virtue, and never resigned themselves to simply facilitating the pursuit of self-interest and hoping that the constant, unbridled clashing of narrow interests would produce the public interest.

Thus, government itself was not the source of public virtue; instead, the promotion of virtue was a function of the primary institutions of society—family, schools, communities, and churches. Reason made clear the importance of public spiritedness and concern for others in a system of self-government, but reason alone could not provide the motivation and commitment to ensure that public virtue would flourish. These values were to be taught and reinforced in the home and from the pulpit, in schools and on election day.

Religion was especially important to the development of a republican culture. The general Judeo-Christian tradition permeated American life. There were strong sentiments of mission, a belief that this pristine land had been set apart and preserved for a chosen people, and faith that America "was not only a destined nation, but a redeeming nation."[3] There was a general consensus that Christian values provided the basis for civil society. Religious leaders had contributed to the political discourse of the Revolution, and the Bible was the most widely read and cited text. Religion, the Founders believed, fostered republicanism and was therefore central to the life of the new nation.

VIRTUE AND RELIGION

For many Americans, the Bible was the primary source for their idea of virtue. The principles articulated there had been spread to a wider audience by the Renaissance and the Reformation. The most immediate motivating forces for public virtue were the Christian belief in benevolence, the Golden Rule, service, and the spiritual transformation that the Puritan movement produced in England—the requirement to live outside one's self in genuine love for others. More than "public regardedness," public virtue was the application of these principles by a Christian people to the society in which they lived.

Puritan ideas spread far beyond New England. Most of the Founders were raised under an omnipresent and potent Protestant/ Puritan ethic. Classical ideas and language were, of course, part of colonial political thought, but they were often infused with a new depth of meaning through religious association. More often than not, even if specific language was drawn from the classical tradition, it was interpreted under the influence of biblical prophets.

Puritanism incorporated the use of reason and moral theology in calling for involvement in good works and strenuous daily effort in behalf of God, man, and self. The idea of virtuous participation in church and state became particularly pronounced. As Puritan spokesman Richard Steele had contended in 1668, "Every man should be of some use in the *Body Politick* as well as in the Body Mistical, or else he is but an Artificial Member, a mere wooden leg"; consequently, "when a man brings no good or profit to the Church or Common-wealth, that's one of *no* calling." Man in his daily activities ought to "make a suitable return of honor and service unto God" by being involved with "The Public Good" and service to "his generation."[4] Given this attitude, historian Ernest Tuveson concluded that the dominant philosophy in early American Christianity was the idea that God was "redeeming both individual souls and society in parallel course."[5] Perry Miller has pointed out that the religious revivals that from time to time enlivened American religious expression were stimulated by the proposition that both men's souls and the larger community were in need of redemption.[6] The godly society needed a virtuous citizenry committed to the promotion of civic responsibility. Furthermore, the idea came to be accepted that *private* virtue must precede *public* virtue. Public virtue was simply the extension of private virtue into public affairs. Man's willingness to sacrifice his immediate self-interest on behalf of the community, his desire to serve the public and to participate in its activities—indeed, even that revolutionary spirit necessary to bring political independence—had their origin in private virtue.

Religion merged classical and biblical virtue by infusing certain ideals and institutions with a sense of the "sacred": there was a "sacred" aura to the Declaration of Independence and later to the

Constitution.[7] During the War of Independence, ministers and political leaders alike called Americans to arms as "the armies of Israel" and in the name of God. Deep in the emotional content of the American tradition was the idea that the colonization and development of the country carried with it a sacred mission. Like individuals, nations were to be held accountable for their actions at a final judgment. The American colonies were commonly referred to as "a city set upon a hill to shine for all the world to see."[8]

Long before the Revolution ever took place, the term "liberty" had taken a sacred connotation and had become part of the idea of virtue. The seeds of freedom had been fertilized with the Reformation, took root in the Puritan revolution, and blossomed in the settlement of the American colonies. "The most powerful single force for freedom in early America," argued Clinton Rossiter, "was the devotion to liberty in the colonial mind."[9] That force was based on the ultimate value of each individual. The philosophy of the Declaration, the basic concepts and unique features undergirding the Revolution—covenant and contract, higher law, inalienable rights, human dignity, and virtue—were all primarily the product of the evolution of American Christianity, particularly Puritanism. American Christianity, with its Judaic influence, was not just compatible with the philosophy that energized men to love freedom or that made them see themselves as heirs of human dignity, subject to law higher than the state; it was primarily responsible for the philosophy. Its strength came from the general belief in its sacredness, its divine nature. It gave man an orientation toward something higher than himself. Human dignity gained its primary force in America from the belief that man was made for eternity, that he had some share in an essence more than human, and that his freedom was divinely ordained.

A religious revival that swept through the colonies four decades before the War of Independence helped promote this idea. Beginning in Georgia, the "Great Awakening" soon spread throughout New England. Alan Heimert and Perry Miller suggest that this movement "marked America's final break with the Middle Ages and her entry into a new intellectual age in the church and society."[10] A new vocabulary, a new thought, a new ideology linking freedom with personal and civic virtue—indeed, a "republican" ideology was being forged from American religion.

It was bolstered by the ideas of British dissenters and libertarians as well as the New World experience itself. There was also a renewed reference to the Puritan past. The Great Awakening was a call for freedom, virtue, and spiritual rejuvenation. It proved to be a catalyst to the growth of both "democratic" and "revolutionary" sentiments in the colonies.

George Whitefield, an itinerant English minister who stirred American audiences with his sermons, called for a return to a "vital religion" and a repudiation of the corrupt and decadent establishment. He and others during the Great Awakening helped spread republican and Revolutionary vocabulary to the masses. "Looking to the New Testament as their model," wrote Harry S. Stout, "the revivalists rediscovered the effectiveness of extemporaneous address in their struggle against the Standing Order."[11] Armed with scriptures and personal charisma, revivalists such as Jonathan Edwards helped provide "pre-Revolutionary America with a radical, even democratic, social and political ideology, an evangelical religion [which] embodied, and inspired, a thrust toward American nationalism."[12]

Revivalistic oratory and technique, as developed by Whitefield, Edwards, and the rest, was different from the usual church sermons of the day. The revivalists were independent of local ministerial rule and their listeners were generally not their parishioners. They organized voluntary public meetings and relied on common, everyday language to reach their audiences.[13]

Before the French and Indian War most Americans were content with their place in the British empire. Revivalist ministers had condemned the luxury and vice that, as they saw it, was corrupting the mother country; but they did not explicitly advocate a war for independence. After 1763 disgruntled Americans drew on that already developed "language" when calling for a revitalized virtue. Patriot spokesmen—some leading ministers included—condemned imperial policy and warned that the colonies were being enslaved by an unfeeling Parliament. They combined the spoken word with such communal rituals as "voting, militia musters and economic associations." This combination created a "collective conscience"—in Virginia, for example, between the gentry and the evangelicals that fostered unity by calling for a common defense.[14]

Another means by which republican ideology was developed

and communicated to the body of Virginians—especially the "humbler ranks" to whom, according to Rhys Isaac, "the pamphlets were rarely addressed"—were the events at "court-day." These monthly meetings brought people together for what turned out to be lessons in civic virtue—legal instruction, participation, and social interaction. Isaac writes that "it was in its monthly concourse at the courthouse that [the] Virginia community was most fully embodied and represented, in ranked order, to itself."[15] It was at these community meetings with their ceremonial forms that the people became acquainted and involved with the local community and the dispensation of justice. The renewal of the county's *commission of the peace* was feted with an elaborate round of oath taking by public officials, and there was the swearing in of juries and participation in elections by the voting freemen. After the court proceedings were festivities usually lasting far into the afternoon that included congenial conversation, the exchange of news and opinions, and an occasional discourse on a subject by a prominent member of the community.[16]

In Virginia and throughout the colonies, it was "republican language" that dramatized events, solidified thought, and forged the forces of revolution. And it was the concept of virtue that laced the republican language with emotional content, ideological zeal, and near-universal meaning. Virtue was "at the heart of patriot aspirations," according to Isaac, and "was a program for the preservation and regeneration of society" that engendered a "basis for popular action."[17] "Virtue" became more than a series of personal responsibilities extrapolated from the scriptures and other moral discourse; it became more than self-sacrifice for the good of church and commonwealth.

VIRTUE AND THE AMERICAN REVOLUTION

As the Revolution drew near, appeals to virtue elicited an increasingly emotional response. This was both a cause and a result of growing feelings of alienation from, of disillusionment with, Great Britain. In the past, sermons had paid homage to Britain and the imperial tie through the king; eventually those sentiments were displaced. The emotional attachment that remained was to Britain's past and to the principles of the Glorious Revolution. Modern Britain came to be seen as a prostitution of its great heritage. A king without "kingly virtues," it was often expressed, was only a man. In effect, what was happening in America was a rebirth of the Puritan revolutionary spirit. A second Puritan revolution—or the New World continuation of the original Puritan revolution and the Glorious Revolution—was taking place. The messages of British radicals such as Algernon Sidney, which proclaimed the right of resistance to the abuse of power, were turned into moral mandates. Britain had become corrupted by violating its own constitution, by allowing the continuation of an unrepresentative Parliament, and by a conspiracy to envelop the American colonies.[18]

The colonists not only recoiled from British political corruption, but they feared moral corruption as well. The public vernacular was expressed not merely in terms of virtue against corruption, but good against evil, virtue against vice, and righteousness against sin. If the conflict with Britain was increasingly seen as a moral battle between virtue and corruption, the same concept caused Americans to look inward to their own worthiness. According to Stout, "The Revolution represented a spiritual purge administered to a corrupt established order in the interest of restoring a pure order that would both free the colonists from a decadent oppressor and cleanse their own society."[19]

Many patriots began to wonder whether enough republican virtue was extant in the colonies to complement the righteousness of their cause. There was a nagging source of anxiety among the Americans: "How could they denounce British corruption if their own virtue was questionable?"[20]

For many, religion and republicanism "would work hand in hand to create frugality, honesty, self-denial, and benevolence among the people."[21] This had been the essence of John Winthrop's famous "City upon a Hill" sermon in 1630, and it was expressed in all aspects of Puritan life—not that they or their descendants always achieved it against the corruption of man's "fallen nature," but that they sought for it, often with great diligence. As Gordon Wood has explained: "The Americans would then 'shew to the nations of the earth (what will be a most singular phenomenon) amidst all the jarring interests, subtlety, and rage of politics' that they 'had virtue enough to think of, and to practice these things.' " Thus, the view of America as a city upon a hill "assumed a new republican character."[22] Sermons and histories tended to glorify America's past in superlatives that exaggerated earlier virtues, bringing a connecting link through jeremiads and other means of communication, filling "believers" with a resolve to "return to first principles." "Virtue" and "first principles" were seen as the keys to both the attainment and the preservation of liberty and free government. The Virginia Declaration of Rights of 1776 stated that "no free government, or the blessings of liberty, can be preserved to any people but by a firm adherence to justice, moderation, temperance, frugality and virtue, and by frequent recurrence to fundamental principles." Four years later the Massachusetts Declaration of Rights reaffirmed that a "constant adherence to . . . piety, justice, moderation, temperance, industry and frugality, are absolutely necessary to preserve the advantages of liberty, and to maintain free government."[23]

The rising sense of crisis that culminated in the issuing of the Declaration of Independence produced a ground swell of concern for virtue. "The decade of crisis brought new popularity to the cult of virtue that had long held sway in the colonies," Rossiter observed. "All the familiar techniques that earlier colonists had borrowed from England and converted to their purposes were revived for the emergency."[24] Having wrestled with the issue of independence, John Adams noted that "the Furnace of Affliction produces Refinement in States as well as Individuals." If America was required to "suffer Calamities" in the effort to win its independence, "it will have this good Effect, at least," he reasoned in a letter to his wife on July 3, 1776, "it will inspire Us with many Virtues, which We have not, and correct many Errors, Follies, and Vices, which threaten to disturb, dishonour, and destroy Us."[25]

The concept of virtue, ever widening in scope and inclusiveness, ever drawing men back to look deeply into their own thoughts and motivations, became a regenerating force that led to a moral "revolution" of thought and action—an "awakening and revival of American principles"[26]—before a shot was fired against Britain. Virtue had founded concepts of republicanism upon a moral dimension: only a virtuous people could enjoy the luxury of prolonged freedom. Virtue, wrote Samuel Williams, echoing many of his fellow clergy, "is the most efficacious principle to hold the different parts of the empire together, and to make men good members of the society to which they belong. . . . And so long as this can be kept up, the rulers and the people, by its influence, will be kept in that place, and move in that course, which the laws of their country have assigned them."[27]

During the Revolutionary era there was a clear consensus that a republic, to stand, must house a virtuous, republican people, and that wholesale corruption was the death knell of republicanism. Great emphasis was placed on "virtue" and "character," which, Wood argued, gave a "moral dimension, a utopian depth, to the political separation from England. . . . Americans had come to believe that the Revolution would mean nothing less than a reordering of eighteenth-century society and politics as they had known and despised them—a reordering that was summed up by the conception of Republicanism."[28] The quest for virtue was more than a general undertaking applied to the individual and the operations of society. It was also the basis of an effort to foster the principles and forms of society as had been attempted in Great Britain by the eighteenth-century English radicals who sought to "purify a corrupt constitution."[29] "Few people in history," argued Rossiter, "have been more given to public moralizing, to proclaiming a catalogue of virtues and exhorting one another to exhibit them, than the American colonists."[30]

The emphasis upon public virtue was not so much a collective philosophy—that the individual should be subordinate to the state—but the Christian view that, by purity of soul, man ought voluntarily to live outside himself in genuine interest for the welfare of others and, if the occasion requires, sacrifice his own interests and desires for the general welfare. This submission was not tantamount to merging the individual personality into the system, nor did it threaten the loss of identity. Individualism was at the core of the American concept of virtue. Here political thought viewed the individual as protected by natural and civil rights. If he was prone to sacrifice his self-interest from time to time, this did not involve the sacrificing of his personhood to the state; he was prior to, antecedent to the state.

Revolutionary leaders were hailed for their examples of virtue. Washington was renowned not only for his military prowess, but, as Henry Commager has observed, he was "revered like no other man of his time, in the Old World and the New, as a symbol of nobility and virtue."[31] This was also true of men like Adams, Jefferson, and Madison. They were idolized by their fellow citizens and became legendary as virtuous and unselfish leaders. The symbol that Adams proposed to place on the Great Seal of the United States of America revealed his predilection. He suggested the engraving of Hercules (by Gribelin) "resting on his club with Virtue pointing to her rugged mountain on one hand, persuading him to ascend, and Sloth glancing at her flowery paths of pleasure, wantonly reclining on the ground to seduce him into vice."[32] Jefferson proposed a scene of the Children of Israel directed by Moses with a "cloud by day and a pillar of fire by night"; and Franklin's design proposed Moses extending his hand over the sea, with the waters overwhelming Pharaoh and divine rays extending from heaven. The motto would be "Rebellion to tyrants is obedience to God."[33]

THE FOUNDERS, RELIGION, AND VIRTUE

The Founders as a whole were deeply religious men. Religion played a vital role in most of their lives; it influenced their beliefs and activities, their ideals and hopes. The foundation of their modern republican philosophy was based on a belief in God. Whatever the concepts that blended to form this republican doctrine—the dignity of man, natural law, natural rights, the right of resistance—all were suffused with an aura of the sacred. Many of the Founders were Christian in their persuasion; others remained skeptical of Christ's divinity, though seldom so of the utilitarian nature of his doctrine for republicanism. Others believed in "one God" as Creator of the universe, a God whose providence remained a real force in history. Unfortunately, many of the Founders who believed in this "activist" God are summarily and incorrectly lumped under the general category of "Deists." To Deists, God was a creator of *first instance* and did not now function as an "activist" force in history.

Nevertheless, Deists generally believed in the immortality of the soul and a judgment by God for actions committed in this life. "The probability that we may be called to account hereafter," wrote Thomas Paine, the self-styled Deist, "will, to reflecting minds, have the influence of belief; for it is not our belief or disbelief that can make or unmake the fact. As this is the state we are in, and which it is proper that we should be in, as free agents, it is a fool only, and not the philosopher, nor even the prudent man, that will live as if there was no God."[34]

A fundamental aspect of the religious philosophy of the Founders was their view of the human personality, including the doctrine of the immortal soul and the concept of human dignity. This energized and legitimized the nature of rights and duties, the insistence upon individual worth and responsibility, brotherhood, and charity or love. It is significant how often reference to benevolence or the Golden Rule appears in the words of the American Founders, accompanied by expressions of their belief in God. This concept was the cornerstone in their ideal of virtue. Thus they sound very much like the Renaissance humanists, Latitudinarians, and Cambridge platonists of previous generations. Typical are Madison's statement that "what is here a right towards men is a duty towards the Creator,"[35] and his prayer that there would be erected "one Empire of reason, benevolence and brotherly affection."[36] Jefferson insisted that "there is only one God, and he all perfect; . . . to love God with all thy heart and thy neighbor as thyself is the sum of religion."[37] Indeed, Jefferson wrote, "nature hath implanted in our breasts a love of others, a sense of duty to them, a moral instinct, in short, which prompts us irresistibly to feel and to succor, their distresses."[38]

Thomas Paine affirmed in *The Age of Reason* that "I consider myself in the hands of my Creator." He proclaimed that "To do good is my religion. I believe that religious duties consist in doing justice, loving mercy, and endeavoring to make our fellow creatures happy."[39] Franklin admonished that the most "acceptable service" one can "render to" God "is in doing good to his other children,"[40] that "the Scripture assures me that at the last Day, we shall not be examin'd for what we *thought,* but what we *did;* and our Recommendation will not be that we said *Lord, Lord,* but that we did GOOD to our Fellow Creatures."[41] John Adams's belief was that the concept of "love your neighbor as yourself, and do to others as you would that others should do to you," was "a great principle of the law of nature."[42] "My religion," he emphasized, "is founded on the love of God, and my neighbor."[43] George Washington, in his 1783 parting address to his troops, stated: "I now make it my earnest prayer that God . . . would incline the hearts of the citizens . . . to entertain a brotherly affection for one another, for their fellow citizens of the United States at large, and particularly for their brethren who have served in the field." If Americans did not embrace charity, humility, and mercy, according to Washington, "we can never hope to be a happy nation."[44]

These statements and numerous others like them show the extent to which the Judeo-Christian ethic had permeated the American concept of virtue and was embraced by the Founders. Time and again the Founders referred to what they believed to be an intervening Providence in their behalf. In *Federalist* No. 2, John Jay expressed his pleasure that "Providence" had "in a particular manner blessed" America in its natural attributes and had "been pleased to give this one connected country to one united people descended from the same ancestors, speaking the same language, professing the same religion, attached to the same principles of government, very similar in their manners and customs and who, by their joint counsels, arms, and efforts fighting side by side throughout a long and bloody war, have nobly established general liberty and independence." "It is impossible for the man of pious reflection," wrote Madison in *Federalist* No. 37 concerning the founding of the nation, "not to perceive in it a finger of that Almighty hand which has been so frequently and signally extended to our relief in the critical stages of the Revolution." In fact, "the real wonder," he offered, "is that so many difficulties should have been surmounted with a unanimity almost as unprecedented as it must have been unexpected. It is impossible for any man of candor to reflect on this circumstance without partaking of the astonishment."[45]

Hamilton wrote in the "Letters of Caesar and Cato" in October 1787, "for my own part, I sincerely esteem it a system, which, without the finger of God, never could have been suggested and agreed upon by such a diversity of interests."[46] Washington insisted that the "Supreme Being" had protected "the liberty and happiness of these United States."[47] He frequently referred to the "interposition of Providence," "the interposing Hand of Heaven," and "the Supreme Ruler of the Universe." In discussing the trials that had been weathered by the new nation, he stated emphatically: "The Hand of Providence has been so conspicuous in all this, that he must be worse than an infidel that lacks faith, and more than wicked, that has not gratitude enough to acknowledge his obligations."[48] In his second inaugural address, Jefferson acknowledged, "that Being in whose hands we are, who led our Forefathers as Israel of old, from their native land and planted them in a country flowing with all the necessaries and comforts of life, who has covered our infancy with his providence and our ripe years with His wisdom and power." "In the beginning of the Contest with G[reat] Britain," Franklin had reaffirmed to the Philadelphia Convention, "when we were sensible of danger we had daily prayer in this room for the divine protection. Our prayers . . . were heard, and they were graciously answered . . . the longer I live, the more convincing proofs I see of this truth— *that God governs in the affairs of men.*"[49]

Not only did the American Founders, in general, express a belief in God, they often expressed the idea that virtue or morality needed the fostering care of religion to keep it alive. Religion and belief in God were viewed as essential to the survival of virtue and morality and hence to the perpetuation of republican government. "Few men who cherished virtue as the foundation of liberty," argued Rossiter, "ever doubted that religion was in turn the foundation of virtue."[50] Franklin argued that "the Motives of religion" were essential for the "great proportion of Mankind" to restrain their vices and promote virtue, since few individuals would be virtuous simply from recognizing the advantages of virtuous living. "If men are so wicked as we now see them *with religion*," he queried, "what would they be if *without it.*"[51]

Madison warned that the future of constitutional institutions would be based, not upon the power of the government, but upon the ability of the people to govern themselves. He was convinced that a "belief in a God all Powerful wise and good is so essential to the moral order of the world and to the happiness of man, that arguments which enforce it cannot be drawn from too many sources."[52] "Of all the dispositions and habits that lead to political prosperity," averred George Washington in his 1796 Farewell Address, "reason and experience both forbid us to expect, that national morality can prevail in exclusion of religious principles."[53] "Our Constitution," stressed John Adams, "was made only for a moral and religious people. It is wholly inadequate to the government of any other." "We have no government armed with power capable of contending with human passions unbridled by morality and religion," he stated in October 1798.[54] And

Samuel Adams added, "Revelation assures us that 'Righteousness exalteth a Nation'—Communities are dealt with in this World by the wise and just Ruler of the Universe. He rewards or punishes them according to their general Character. The diminution of publick Virtue is usually attended with that of publick Happiness, and the publick Liberty will not long survive the total Extinction of Morals."[55]

CIVIL RELIGION AND GOVERNMENT

Throughout history, religion has played a central role in ensuring the legitimacy and authority of the state. The Founders of the American republic accepted that tradition in part and in part rejected it. For them, religion helped provide the basis of civil society, but religion was also to be independent of the state. They challenged much of the traditional wisdom of the relationship between religion and government in their attempt to ensure freedom of belief and conscience.

The term *civil religion* has been used to describe the official religion of a given state or political regime. Most frequently, the term is used to describe those of nations of antiquity—including classical Greece and Rome, the Holy Roman Empire, and the unified national church–state systems that emerged out of the Renaissance and Reformation. The term has also been used to describe the system of "established" churches during the American colonial period. Civil religion is also used to describe, in the broadest sense, a people or a nation's "official" or generally accepted dogmas and symbols, inherited and reinforced through indoctrination and socialization.

Still others use civil religion more narrowly to describe a nation or a community's common or unofficial religion. In this context, it is argued that, even though the "religion" is neither specifically organized nor officially established, the generally held beliefs and values that are its expression are integral to the society's culture; therefore, its impact on other groups and formal institutions of society qualify it as a "civil religion." In a system with multiple sectarian religions, this "general religion" will express principles that are promoted by, sanctioned by, or at least amenable to the sects that make up the body of organized, though not official or state, churches. Although this genre of "civil religion" is unofficial, certain aspects of it may become institutional-ized in national rituals, symbols, or shrines. An example of this type of "civil" religion or theology is the "general" or "common" religion of the United States.

From the beginning of American colonization there existed some form of civil religion, a phenomenon that has exerted a profound effect on the development of American republicanism. The existence of a civil religion is not remarkable. The essential point to be developed here is the way in which the Framers integrated their idea of civil religion with the structure of govern-ment they created. The Constitution presupposed a commitment on the part of the people to republican virtues. This, of course, was not enough and the Framers focused their attention on the governing structures and processes that they believed would best secure republican government. But they believed, as Madison put it in *Federalist,* that "A dependence on the people is, no doubt, the primary control on the government." The separation of pow-ers and internal and external controls on the government were also necessary as "auxiliary precautions."[56]

Religion played an important role in the development of American freedom and the rule of law. Both the organized reli-gions and the general religious atmosphere combined to validate law and to enshrine the ideal of responsible freedom. Not only ministers but government leaders incorporated God into the pub-lic philosophy, along with other civil values and rituals. These ideals survived the decline of Puritan zeal and "continued to have a powerful shaping effect on succeeding generations."[57]

It was this general form of religious "feeling" or faith— developed from the Judeo–Christian–Puritan ethic—which, as Alexis de Tocqueville later perceived, was the primary ingredient in developing and sustaining morality, unity, harmony, and co-operation in the American community. It was the basic influence in keeping society from bursting its seams. Its emphasis on moral behavior as a guide for interaction with others allowed social, economic and political exchange to a degree unknown in other countries. It tended to stimulate that kind of responsible behavior that keeps the heady mixture of freedom and democracy within certain bounds so that it does not run away with itself. In short, it helped create a people who could be self-governing.

Some of the American Founders avoided affiliation with the

organized religions of their day. They tended to support a "general" religion in much the same way that Tocqueville later did; and, just as he, they recognized its importance to the health of the republic. Whatever their religious beliefs, there was in evidence a *general religion* that permeated the thought of these early Americans and superimposed over the nation a sort of harmony that superseded the conflict between sects and between the "churched" and the "unchurched." This "general" philosophy or theology included a belief in God, obligations to one's fellowmen, and acceptance of that doctrine Tocqueville was later to emphasize as so critical for citizens of a democratic republic—immortality and a final judgment. It was Franklin who perhaps best outlined the basic aspects of this general "theology" or "philosophy." "Here is my creed," he wrote, "I believe in one God, Creator of the universe. That he governs it by his providence. That he ought to be worshipped. That the most acceptable service we render to him is in doing good to his other children. That the soul of man is immortal, and will be treated with justice in another life respecting its conduct in this. These I take to be the fundamental points of all sound religion."[58]

Jefferson's creed was similar; he championed moral precepts such as loving one's neighbor.[59] In his first inaugural address he extended his hope that "the United States will be enlightened by a benign religion, professed, indeed, and practiced in various forms, yet all of them including honesty, truth, temperance, gratitude, and the love of man; acknowledging and adoring an overruling Providence which by all its dispensations proves that it delights in the happiness of man here and his greater happiness thereafter."[60] So, too, did Thomas Paine express his devotion to God and his "hope for happiness beyond this life,"[61] that the purpose of life was "for our own happiness and His glory," and that he relied upon "his protection both here and hereafter."[62] Samuel Adams referred to these basic concepts as "the religion of America," even, "the religion of all mankind."[63]

While many of the Founders held anticlerical attitudes, they nevertheless saw in religion the basis for self-government. Even if John Adams believed that there had been a certain corruption of Christianity, he accepted the Christian ethic as indispensable to a free and stable society. He, like Jefferson, revered Christianity in its pristine purity as expressed in the New Testament. "The substance of Christianity as I understand it," he wrote, "is eternal and unchangeable and will bear examination forever." He lamented, however, that Christianity had "been mixed with extraneous ingredients which I think will not bear examination and they ought to be separated."[64] Yet, even in its present form, Adams marveled at Christianity's character and salubrious effect. In his diary dated July 26, 1796, he wrote, "The Christian religion is, above all the religions that ever prevailed or existed in ancient or modern times, the religion of wisdom, virtue, equity, and humanity."[65] Again, under the date of August 14, 1796, he wrote of Christianity as a leavening, morally restraining force, while emphasizing the Golden Rule and the doctrine of immortality. In his words one can perceive the importance he placed on Christianity as a means of political socialization:

> One great advantage of the Christian religion is that it brings the great principle of the law of nature and nations—Love your neighbor as yourself, and do to others as you would that others should do to you—to the knowledge, belief, and veneration of the whole people. Children, servants, women, and men, are all professors in the science of public and private morality. No other institution for public and private morality, no other institution for education, no kind of political discipline, could diffuse this necessary kind of information so universally among all ranks and descriptions of citizens. The duties and rights of the man and the citizen are thus taught from early infancy to every creature. The sanctions of a future life are thus added to the observance of civil and political, as well as domestic and private duties. Prudence, justice, temperance, and fortitude, are thus taught to be the means and conditions of future as well as present happiness.[66]

Although Franklin too was sometimes frustrated with the sectarian disputes of his time, he still contended that the Christian system of religion and morality was "the best the world ever saw or is likely to see," and he subscribed to its basic "essentials" which were "to be found in all the religions we had in our country."[67] He regularly paid his "annual subscription for the support of the only Presbyterian minister or meeting we had," and contributed his "mite" to the construction of new churches in Philadelphia, "whatever might be their sect."[68] He saw both denominational religion and "general" religion as salutary for the Republic. In his "Proposals Relating to the Education of Youth in Pennsylvania" (1749) he advocated the study of history that would "afford frequent opportunities of showing the Necessity of a *Public Religion,* from its Usefulness to the Public, the Advantage of a Religious Character Among private Persons; the Mischiefs of Superstition, etc., and the Excellency of the CHRISTIAN RELI-GION above all others Ancient and Modern." According to Franklin, "The general natural tendency of reading good history must be to fix in the minds of youth deep impressions of the beauty and usefulness of virtue of all kinds, public spirit, fortitude, etc."[69]

James Madison described Christianity in 1832 as "the best and purest religion."[70] The next year, Justice Joseph Story called Christianity "the religion of liberty." "In a Republic," Story wrote, "there would seem to be a peculiar propriety in viewing the Christian religion as the great basis on which it [republican liberty] must rest for its support and permanence, if it be what it has ever been deemed by its best friends to be, the religion of liberty. Montesquieu has remarked that the Christian religion is a stranger to mere despotic power."[71]

If Jefferson was "unchurched" because of his philosophical and theological quarrel with some of the clergy, he remained devout in his belief in God, unmoving in his admiration for the "pure" doctrines of Christ as moral guidelines. Jefferson was far more impressed with the Founder of Christianity than he was with many of His modern followers. "Of the systems of morality ancient or modern, which have come under my observation," he wrote, "none appear to me so pure as that of Jesus. He who follows this steadily need not, I think, be uneasy, although he cannot comprehend the subtleties and mysteries erected in His doctrine by those who, calling themselves His special followers and favorites, would make Him come into the world to lay snares for all understanding but theirs."[72] He was convinced that the system of morality as advocated by Christ was "more perfect than those of any of the ancient philosophers." Morality as Jesus taught it, "freed from the corruptions of latter times, is far superior."[73] Jefferson preferred to return in doctrine to the "unlettered Apostles, the Apostolic Fathers, and the Christians of the first century."[74] In a letter to Dr. Joseph Priestly, Jefferson called Christian philosophy "the most sublime and benevolent but the most perverted system that ever shone on man."[75] And to his friend, Dr. Benjamin Rush, he wrote: "Not withstanding these disadvantages, a system of morals is presented to us, which, if filled up in the style and spirit of the rich fragments he left us, would be the most perfect and sublime that has ever been taught by man."[76]

Jefferson saw the doctrines of Christianity as being utilitarian and universal in application, having the potential of uniting all mankind in "one family in the bonds of life, peace, common wants, and common aids."[77] Jefferson, who had questions concerning the divinity of Christ, still contended that "had the doctrines of Jesus been preached always as pure as they came from his lips, the whole civilized world would now have been Christian."[78] Although Jefferson respected Christianity as an unequaled moral doctrine, his concern for individual liberty led him to champion religious freedom. Freedom of belief was bound up with other personal freedoms; and while a commitment to Christian beliefs was part of his political culture, he championed efforts such as the Virginia Statute of Religious Freedom as essential in assuring individual liberty. "I have sworn upon the alter of God," he wrote, "eternal hostility against every form of tyranny over the mind of man."[79] For Jefferson, pure Christianity posed no such threat.

CIVIL RELIGION AND THE NATIONAL FUTURE

When the youthful French aristocrat Alexis de Tocqueville visited America in 1831–32 he claimed to have found there a "general Christianity" which, far from having lost its import with the coming of the constitutional republic, was more essential than ever before. In his view a modern democratic republic needed a "civil religion"; indeed, needed it more than any other kind of government. Tocqueville's concern with the spread of democracy in his time led him to contemplate the importance of culture and the cultural attributes that he came to perceive as necessary for the survival of freedom. Tocqueville was particularly interested in the impact of religion on modern democracy. He leaves the truth or falsity of religious belief to another realm, yet he does not undercut religion nor does he attack its spiritual doctrines. His point is that religion is important in utilitarian ways. He suggests that people can be motivated by the mind as well as the heart, that moral precepts advocated by religion may be promoted because they are practical and beneficial.[80]

Tocqueville's central concern in studying modern democracies was the manners, the customs, and the character of the people in a given polity. He identified these as "the whole moral and intellectual condition of a people" because as far as he was concerned they revealed more about the character of a social system than any other single factor.[81] Like the American Founders before him, he came to believe that a democratic republic required a special kind of people. "The importance of customs," he concluded, "is a common truth to which study and experience incessantly direct our attention."[82] The "manners" or "customs"—"the moral and intellectual condition"—of the people, emphasized Tocqueville, are more important than their "physical circumstances," even their "laws." "I am convinced," he wrote, "that the most advantageous situation and the best possible laws cannot maintain a constitution in spite of the customs of a country; while the latter may turn to some advantage the most unfavorable positions and the worst laws."[83]

Tocqueville came to see an inseparable relationship between the American republic and the body of those universal principles that, having emerged from the evolution of modern Christianity, had become generally accepted beliefs. Those beliefs would in turn help the people exercise self-restraint. Instead of the state controlling the people and thereby likely becoming tyrannical, the people—imbued with a sense of civic virtue—would restrain themselves. Without restraints, freedom is likely to degenerate into chaos and disorder. Tocqueville emphasized the importance of religion and its salutary effects on a system of freedom. "Liberty regards religion as its companion in all its battles and its triumphs, as the cradle of its infancy and the divine source of its claims. It considers religion as the safeguard of morality, and morality as the best security of law and the surest pledge of the duration of freedom."[84] Religion, he believed, was essential so that popular government could be tempered and moderated.

Religion promotes self-restraint, both in the rulers and the ruled, and mitigates those individualist tendencies that destroy compassion and philanthropy and work to atomize society. At the same time, it supports the maintenance of responsible freedom. This allows moral suasion, the influence of faith and common sense, to become forces of human motivation. Without this well from which democracies must drink to perpetuate themselves, societal rules and regulations will eventually become relative and confusing. The loss of religion and a moral structure in a democratic society is tantamount to the loss of balance and stability. "I doubt," surmised Tocqueville, "whether man can ever support at the same time complete religious independence [absence] and entire political freedom."[85]

Therefore, a democratic republic was in *more*—not *less*—need of a "civil religion" or theology than an autocratic society. "Despotism may govern without faith, but liberty cannot. Religion is much more necessary in the republic . . . than in the monarchy . . . *it is more needed in democratic republics than in any others. How is it possible that society should escape destruction if the moral tie is not strengthened in proportion as the political tie is relaxed? And what can be done with a people who are their own masters if they are not submissive to the Deity?*"[86]

In spite of the numerous religious sects Tocqueville found in America, he perceived there to be a "general" Christianity, a commonly accepted public philosophy, one which he found highly salutary for the republic. He believed that some form of public philosophy was necessary for any degree of unity and cooperation in a democracy, and that this general public philosophy with its Christian foundation formed the peculiar character of democracy in America. "Christianity," he wrote, "has . . . retained a strong hold on the public mind in America; and I would more particularly remark that its sway is not only that of a philosophical doctrine which has been adopted upon inquiry, but of a religion which is believed without discussion. In the United States, Christian sects are infinitely diversified and perpetually modified; but Christianity itself is an established and irresistible fact, which no one undertakes either to attack or to defend."[87] Although "the sects that exist in the United States" were "innumerable," Tocqueville saw them all resting on the moral foundation that ancient Christianity had bequeathed them. "They all differ in respect to the worship which is due to the Creator; but they all agree in respect to the duties which are due from man to man. Each sect adores the Deity in its own peculiar manner, but all sects preach the same moral law in the name of God." They were "comprised within the great unity of Christianity, and Christian morality is everywhere the same." Therefore, Tocqueville spoke of the "Gospel" in terms of the "general relations of men to God and each other, beyond which it . . . imposes no point of faith."[88]

Tocqueville returned time and again to a contemplation of the relationship between the nature of man, religion, and political institutions. "On my arrival" in America, he wrote, "the religious aspect of the country was the first thing that struck my attention; and the longer I stayed there, the more I perceived the great political consequences resulting from this new state of things."[89] In a nutshell, the colonists had "brought with them into the New World a form of Christianity which I cannot better describe than by styling it a democratic and republican religion. This contributed powerfully to the establishment of a republic and a democracy in public affairs."[90] In Americans, he had found a "republican" people who could coalesce the spirit of religion and the spirit of freedom: "In America religion is the road to knowledge and the observance of the divine laws leads man to civil freedom."[91] Not only did Tocqueville see religion as "one of the most prominent . . . causes to which the maintenance of the political institutions of the Americans is attributable," but he also observed that "religion is not less useful to each citizen than to the whole state. The Americans show by their practice that they feel the high necessity of imparting morality to democratic communities by means of religion."[92] "The Americans," he explained, "combine the notions of Christianity and of liberty so intimately in their minds that it is impossible to make them conceive the one without the other. . . . I have known of societies formed by Americans to send out ministers of the Gospel into the new Western states, to found schools and churches there, lest religion should be allowed to die away in those remote settlements, and the rising states be less fitted to enjoy free institutions than the people from whom they came."[93] While all Americans might not be devotees of religion, they nevertheless, he believed, "hold it to be indispensable to the maintenance of republican institutions."[94]

Both the Framers of the American Constitution and Tocqueville recognized the interaction of political culture and governing institutions. Virtue, freedom, and enlightened self-interest were all at the heart of the "new science of politics" that had developed in America. The Revolution tested the strength of the American commitment to these values, and while their experiences and those of other political regimes that the Framers studied were sobering, the American Founders maintained their belief that self-government was possible. They gave careful attention to the structure and powers of the government they formed, but they believed that this framework was to rest on a firm basis of civic virtue. They believed that a republic could not be assured solely by the checking and balancing of political institutions and processes but also required a commitment on the part of the citizenry to self-government. For the Framers and many like Tocqueville who followed them, religion played a central role in developing that commitment.

Notes

1. *Federalist* 57:350.

2. *Federalist* 51:322.

3. Robert Nisbet, *History of the Idea of Progress* (New York: Basic Books, 1980), 197.

4. Richard Steele, *The Husbandman's Calling* (London, 1668), 7–8, 15, 234 (italics added).

5. Ernest Tuveson, *Redeemer Nation* (Chicago: University of Chicago Press, 1974), 12; Nathan O. Hatch, *The Sacred Cause of Liberty* (New Haven, Conn.: Yale University Press, 1977) builds upon Tuveson's work; see also Conrad Cherry, ed., *God's New Israel* (Englewood Cliffs, N.J.: Prentice-Hall, 1971); and William A. Clebsch, *From Sacred to Profane America* (New York: Harper and Row, 1968).

6. Perry Miller, *The Life of the Mind in America: From the Revolution to the Civil War* (New York: Harcourt, Brace, and World, 1965), 10.

7. Catherine L. Albanese, *Sons of the Fathers* (Philadelphia: Temple University Press, 1976).

8. Ralph Ketcham, *James Madison* (New York: Macmillan, 1971), 47–48.

9. Clinton Rossiter, *The First American Revolution* (New York: Harcourt, Brace, and World, 1956), 191.

10. Alan Heimert and Perry Miller, eds., *The Great Awakening: Documents Illustrating the Crisis and Its Consequences* (Indianapolis: Bobbs-Merrill, 1967), xiv–xv.

11. Harry S. Stout, "Religion, Communications, and the Ideological Origins of the American Revolution," *William and Mary Quarterly* 34 (1977): 528–29.

12. Alan E. Heimert, *Religion and the American Mind* (Cambridge, Mass.: Harvard University Press, 1966), viii.

13. Stout, "Religion, Communications, and the Ideological Origins of the American Revolution," 527, 528, 530.

14. See Rhys Isaac's, "Preachers and Patriots: Popular Culture and the Revolution in Virginia," in Alfred Young, ed., *The American Revolution* (Dekalb: Northern Illinois University Press, 1976), 125–56.

15. Rhys Isaac, "Dramatizing the Ideology of Revolution: Popular Mobilization in Virginia 1774–1776," *William and Mary Quarterly* 33 (1976): 364–65.

16. Ibid., 369.

17. Ibid., 368.

18. H. Trevor Colbourn, "John Dickinson, Historical Revolutionary," *Pennsylvania Magazine of History and Biography* 83 (1959): 283.

19. Stout, "Religion, Communications, and the Ideological Origins of the American Revolution," 523. See Page Smith, ed., *Religious Origins of the American Revolution* (Missoula, Mont.: Scholars Press, 1976), an anthology of documents (such as excerpts from Calvin's *Institutes*) with Smith's running commentary on how historians have too often missed religious influences on American Revolutionary ideology.

20. Isaac, "Preachers and Patriots," 145.

21. Gordon S. Wood, *The Creation of the American Republic, 1776–1787* (Chapel Hill: University of North Carolina Press, 1969), 118.

22. Ibid.

23. Bernard Schwartz, ed., *The Roots of the Bill of Rights,* 5 vols. (1971; reprint, New York: Chelsea House, 1980), 2:234 (Virginia), 2:343 (Massachusetts).

24. Clinton Rossiter, *Political Thought of the American Revolution* (New York: Harcourt, Brace, and World, 1963), 200.

25. Letter to Abigail Adams, in L. H. Butterfield, Marc Friedlaender, and Mary-Jo Kline, eds., *The Book of Abigail and John: Selected Letters of the Adams Family, 1762–1784* (Cambridge, Mass.: Harvard University Press, 1975), 140.

26. Charles Francis Adams, ed., *The Works of John Adams,* 10 vols. (Boston: Little, Brown and Co., 1850–56), 10:284.

27. Samuel Williams, *Discourse on Love of Our Country* (Salem, 1775), 13–14.

28. Wood, *Creation of the American Republic,* 47–48.

29. Bernard Bailyn, *The Ideological Origins of the American Revolution* (Cambridge, Mass.: Harvard University Press, Belknap Press, 1967), 283.

30. Rossiter, *First American Revolution,* 226, 221.

31. Henry Steele Commager, "Brilliant Originals. Whatever happened to the political genius that founded America?" *Washington Post Magazine,* October 10, 1982, 33.

32. Charles Francis Adams, ed., *Familiar Letters of John Adams and His Wife, Abigail Adams, during the Revolution* (Boston: Hurd and Houghton, 1876), 210–11.

33. Richard S. Patterson and Richardson Dougall, *The Eagle and the Shield: A History of the Great Shield of the United States* (Washington D.C.: Department of State, 1978); Gaillard Hunt, "The Seal of the United States: How It Was Developed and Adopted" (Washington, D.C.: Department of State, 1892).

34. Thomas Paine, *The Age of Reason* (London: Watts, 1938), 106–9.

35. James Madison, "Remonstrance," in Saul K. Padover, ed., *The Complete Madison: His Basic Writings* (New York: Harper and Row, 1953), 300.

36. Gaillard Hunt, ed., *The Writings of James Madison,* 9 vols. (New York: G. P. Putnam's Sons, 1900–1910), 6:69.

37. A. A. Lipscomb and A. E. Bergh, eds., *The Writings of Thomas Jefferson,* 20 vols. (Washington, D.C.: Thomas Jefferson Memorial Association, 1903–4), 15:384.

38. Ibid., 14:139–43.

39. Paine, *Age of Reason,* 1.

40. Jared Sparks, ed., *The Works of Benjamin Franklin,* 10 vols. (Boston: Hilliard, Gray, 1836–40), 10:423.

41. L. Jesse Lemisch, ed., *Benjamin Franklin: The Autobiography and Other Writings* (New York: New American Library, 1961), 320.

42. L. H. Butterfield, ed., *The Adams Papers: Diary and Autobiography of John Adams,* 4 vols. (Cambridge, Mass.: Harvard University Press, Belknap Press, 1961), 3:240–41.

43. Adams, *Works of John Adams,* 6:234.

44. Saul K. Padover, ed., *The Washington Papers* (New York: Harper and Row, 1955), 257–62.

45. *Federalist* 2:38, 37:230–31.

46. Paul L. Ford, *Essays on the Constitution of the United States* (Brooklyn, N.Y.: Historical Printing Club, 1892), 251–52.

47. John C. Fitzpatrick, ed., *The Writings of George Washington,* 39 vols. (1932–45; reprint, Washington, D.C.: Government Printing Office, 1970), 27:116, 249, 281.

48. Ibid., 12:343.

49. Max Farrand, ed., *The Records of the Federal Convention of 1787,* rev. ed., 4 vols. (New Haven, Conn.: Yale University Press, 1966), 1:451.

50. Rossiter, *Political Thought of the American Revolution,* 220–21.

51. Albert Henry Smyth, ed., *The Writings of Benjamin Franklin,* 10 vols. (1905–7; reprint, New York: Macmillan, 1970), 9:521–22 (italics in the original).

52. Hunt, *Writings of James Madison,* 9:230.

53. George de Huszar et al., *Basic American Documents* (Ames, Iowa: Littlefield, Adams, 1953), 2:108–9.

54. Adams, *Works of John Adams,* 9:229.

55. Adams to John Scollay, April 30, 1776, in Alonzo Cushing, ed., *The Writings of Samuel Adams,* 4 vols. (New York: G. P. Putnam's Sons, 1904–8), 3:286.

56. *Federalist* 51:322.

57. Sydney E. Ahlstrom, "The Puritan Ethic and the Spirit of American Democracy," in George L. Hunt, ed., *Calvinism and the Political Order* (Philadelphia: Westminster Press, 1965), 97–98.

58. Smyth, *Writings of Benjamin Franklin,* 10:84.

59. John Dewey, *The Living Thoughts of Thomas Jefferson* (New York: Longmans, Green and Co., 1940), 102.

60. Saul K. Padover, ed., *The Complete Jefferson* (Freeport, N.Y.: Books For Libraries, 1969), 385–87.

61. Thomas Paine, *The Age of Reason* (New York: G. P. Putnam's Sons, 1890), 21.

62. Thomas Paine, "Of the Religion of Deism," in Philip S. Foner, ed., *The Life and Major Writings of Thomas Paine* (New York: Citadel Press, 1945), 798.

63. William V. Wells, *The Life of Samuel Adams,* 2d ed. (Freeport, N.Y.: Books For Libraries, 1969), 3:23.

64. Lester J. Cappon, ed., *The Adams–Jefferson Letters, 1812–1826,* 2 vols. (Chapel Hill: University of North Carolina Press, 1959), 2:608.

65. Adams, *Works of John Adams,* 3:421.

66. Ibid., 423–24.

67. Smyth, *Writings of Benjamin Franklin,* 15:324.

68. Ibid.

69. Ibid., 2:392–93.

70. Hunt, *Writings of James Madison,* 1:21.

71. Joseph Story, *Commentaries on the Constitution of the United States,* 2 vols. (Boston: Little, Brown & Co., 1858), 1:319.

72. Dewey, *Living Thoughts of Thomas Jefferson,* 103. Lipscomb and Bergh, *Writings of*

Thomas Jefferson, 12:345–46. See also Adrienne Koch, *The Philosophy of Thomas Jefferson* (New York: Columbia University Press, 1943), 26.

73. Dewey, *Living Thoughts of Thomas Jefferson,* 108. See also the letter to John Adams, July 5, 1814, in Lipscomb and Bergh, *Writings of Thomas Jefferson,* 14:147–51; and letter to Charles Thomson, January 9, 1816, in Paul L. Ford, ed., *The Writings of Thomas Jefferson,* 10 vols. (New York: G. P. Putnam's Sons, 1892–99), 10:5–6 (italics in the original).

74. Letter to John Adams, October 13, 1813, in Lipscomb and Bergh, *Writings of Thomas Jefferson,* 13:390.

75. Letter to Dr. Joseph Priestly, March 21, 1801, in ibid., 10: 228–29, 15:323.

76. Letter to Dr. Benjamin Rush, April 21, 1803, in ibid., 379–85.

77. Paul L. Ford, ed., *The Works of Thomas Jefferson,* 10 vols. (New York: G. P. Putnam's Sons, 1905), 9:463.

78. Letter to Dr. Benjamin Waterhouse, June 26, 1822, in Lipscomb and Bergh, *Writings of Thomas Jefferson,* 15:383–85. In other writings, Jefferson takes the position against the divinity of Christ. He rejected such doctrines as "immaculate conception" and "His corporal presence in the Eucharist." Cappon, *Adams–Jefferson Letters,* 384.

79. Lipscomb and Bergh, *Writings of Thomas Jefferson,* 15:323.

80. Alexis de Tocqueville, *Democracy in America,* ed. Phillips Bradley, 2 vols. (New York: Vintage Books, 1958), 2:23–24.

81. Ibid., 1:310.

82. Ibid., 334.

83. Ibid.

84. Ibid., 46.

85. Ibid., 2:23.

86. Ibid., 1:318 (italics added).

87. Ibid., 2:6–7.

88. Ibid., 1:314–15, 2:24.

89. Ibid., 1:319.

90. Ibid., 311.

91. Ibid., 43 (italics in the original).

92. Ibid., 2:152–53.

93. Ibid., 1:317.

94. Ibid., 316.

John P. Diggins is a native San Franciscan. He graduated from the University of California, Berkeley, in 1957, went on for his M.A. at San Francisco State University, and then a Ph.D. from the University of Southern California in 1964. He joined the faculty of San Francisco State soon after finishing his dissertation. Currently a professor of history at the University of California, Irvine, he has been teaching at Irvine since 1969.

Diggins is an intellectual historian of great breadth whose books and articles have ranged from discussions of Thoreau and Marx to the American view of Mussolini and fascism. His concern in *The American Left in the Twentieth Century* for "the mind and moral temper of a generation as it arises from concrete historical experience" rather than "the disembodied 'history of ideas' " was carried into *The Lost Soul of American Politics* (New York: Basic Books, 1984). J. R. Pole of St. Catherine's College, Oxford, called this study "the most ambitious and in my judgment the most important contribution to the history of political ideas in America to have appeared for several years." In it Diggins counters those like J. G. A. Pocock who have emphasized the impact of Renaissance notions of civic virtue on American thought. Calvinism and liberalism, asserts Diggins, have been more crucial components of the American tradition. He suggests that liberalism and an attachment to individualism and self-interest grew even as the Calvinistic strain of self-denial and humility shrank over time.

As Professor Diggins admonishes in the essay printed here, it would be difficult, perhaps impossible, for us to return to "first principles." And even if we could the Constitution might not be a good starting point. To some American intellectuals the Constitution has not been the best expression of our political genius or higher moral purpose.

V

RECOVERING "FIRST PRINCIPLES": CRITICAL PERSPECTIVES ON THE CONSTITUTION AND THE FATE OF CLASSICAL REPUBLICANISM

★

John Patrick Diggins

As Americans celebrate the Bicentennial of the Constitution, we have heard a plethora of platitudes honoring the document as the quintessential statement of political wisdom and the foundation of modern freedom. Such rhetoric and rituals are perhaps necessary in any given society. Even so, from the eighteenth to the twentieth century the Constitution has had its share of critics, and the criticisms pertain not only to the alleged theoretical and structural flaws in the Constitution, but also to the fate of classical republicanism in American politics.

In the Atlantic tradition of classical republicanism it was assumed that for a republican polity to survive it must engage in a periodic return to its "first principles." Supposedly, a frequent recurrence to the ideas and institutions that made republican liberty possible would provide a beacon of hope and a source of knowledge, a Machiavellian *ricorso* enabling us to avoid the fate of Old World republics which, having lost sight of their original ideals of "civic virtue," had succumbed to inevitable corruption and decline as the pursuit of private interest replaced the ideal of the public good, *res publica*. In this respect a republic owes its meaning to its origin and creation, to the act of founding that signifies the highest moment when ideals were formulated in words, enacted into deeds, and institutionalized in the structure and function of government. By the same token a republic's future depends upon its knowledge of the past because the study of history can help defeat the tyranny of time, that inexorable process of change and decay that threatens to render all things under the sun perishable.

In view of the classical imperative to return to the past, it is curious that so many outstanding American thinkers found little inspiration in returning to the Constitution and the political principles enunciated at the Philadelphia Convention. Many intellectuals and statesmen saw the Constitution itself as highly problematic. In their view the Constitution frustrated rather than fulfilled the ideals of classical republicanism. If the spirit of classical republicanism did indeed fail to survive the development of American political culture, what role did the Constitution play in all of this?

FEDERALISTS AND ANTIFEDERALISTS

The first generation of American political thinkers who grappled with the problem of preserving republican ideals split into two sharply divided camps, the Federalists and the Antifederalists. And here the preoccupation with power that had agitated the American mind at the time of the Revolution seems to have persisted into the Constitutional era. The burden of the Federalists was to explain to their critics how republican liberty could be preserved in a system of government that would transfer power from the local to the national level. The Federalists could guarantee that the familiar institutional forms of republicanism were being preserved, namely, the principles of mixed government, separation of power, checks and balances, rotation in office, and the like. But the *Federalist* authors would not guarantee that other features of classical republicanism could or even should be incorporated into the Constitution, especially the assumption that the American republic must depend upon a virtuous citizenry, or that the majority can be trusted to preserve its own liberties, or that the only tyranny to be feared was that of executive usurpation, or that all power should be distrusted as incompatible with liberty. Nor would the *Federalist* authors, despite the homage they paid to the language of republicanism, reassure their opponents that the proposed Constitution had a direct lineal ancestry to the older republics of classical antiquity or even a rough reflection of the ideas of Montesquieu and the republican theories of the Enlightenment. For the *Federalist* writers saw themselves engaged in a "novel" experiment with politics and power, one that would establish what Madison called a "system without precedent ancient or modern." Why, complained Hamilton, should the Constitution be rejected simply because the theories underlying it are "new?"[1]

What was new in the thoughts of Hamilton and Madison was precisely the set of propositions that the Antifederalists sought to refute: that a republic can be large and expansive rather than, as Montesquieu had warned, small and simple; that the people can be diverse and factious rather than cohesive and homogeneous; that the system of representation can be intricate and distant yet not alienate the people from government; that commerce and luxury posed no clear danger, as David Hume had taught, to virtue and morality; that the new Constitution would overcome the debilities of the Articles of Confederation and resolve once and for all the source of national sovereignty; that there is more to fear from popular majorities in the House than from an aristocratic elite in the Senate; and that power can be controlled with what Patrick Henry dismissed as "your specious, imaginary imbalances, your rope-dancing, chain-rattling, ridiculous ideal checks and balances."[2] Henry, George Mason, and other Antifederalists were convinced that the consolidation of power in the national government threatened the liberty of people in the respective states, particularly when the Constitution contained no bill of rights.

When we consider the reasoning of Hamilton and Madison together with the pleas of Henry and other Antifederalists, it is not difficult to understand why republicanism could not enjoy political authority: it had no moral capacity to command obedience. The Federalists, recognizing that men would respond only to those ideas that reflected their immediate interests, had doubts that the nation's public good could ever be realized.[3] Hamilton did hold out some hope that a small number of men of wealth and talent could be induced to devote their services to the nation as administrators acting from reasons of fame and honor. But the Antifederalists, who could only see in Hamilton's hopes a sinister plot aiming at aristocratic domination, also saw little chance that either the few or the many could transcend interest and power and regard the protection of national welfare as the highest ideal. Thus for Patrick Henry the public good was simply that which was good for the state of Virginia, and he assumed it was an act of political virtue to remain suspicious of anything that might hinder local interests, rights, and privileges. The liberty he and many other Antifederalists spoke of was essentially "negative liberty," to use Isaiah Berlin's term, the liberty to resist the encroachments of political authority and state power, the liberty to be one's own master, the liberty to be autonomous and self-reliant.[4]

Nowhere was the tension between republicanism and liberalism more acutely felt than in the ideas and political career of Thomas Jefferson. Even though, as Joyce Appleby has shown, Jefferson cannot be incorporated within the "Country–Court" categories on the assumption that, like his English rural counterparts, he resisted political democracy and the emergence of commercial society, he did long for that lost world perhaps because he had done much to destroy it. Jefferson retained both a liberal predilection for unbounded individualism and natural rights and a classical predilection for closely defined communities and local civic responsibility. Thus, the author of the Declaration of Independence could wax Lockean about preserving the natural rights of life, liberty, and property against the power of government and then proceed to augment the authority of government and violate a strict construction of the Constitution with the Louisiana Purchase and nationally imposed embargoes, both of which undermined his cherished principles of "least" government, state sovereignty, and the fecundity of natural society. But against such centralizing tendencies, Jefferson, in his later post-presidential career, would invoke his idea of a "ward system," where he waxed classical and wanted to see active citizen participation in local politics on the assumption that the immediate polity nurtures responsible conduct. "Each ward," Jefferson wrote in 1824, "would thus be a small republic within itself." Jefferson also wrote privately that "Greece was the first of civilized nations which presented examples of what men should be." In *On Revolution,* Hannah Arendt makes much of Jefferson's belated classical nostalgia, implying that he almost felt guilty about abandoning the "revolutionary spirit" of 1776, America's "lost treasure." But Jefferson was liberal even within his classical mode, because his passion for small wards concerned less the noble life of political action than the entrepreneurial life of freedom from all direction:

> Every state is again divided into counties, each to take care of what lies within local bounds; each county again into townships or wards, to manage minute details; and every ward into farms, to be governed by its individual proprietor. Were we directed from Washington when to sow, and when to reap, we should soon want bread. It is by this partition of cares, descending in gradation from the general to the particular, that the mass of human affairs may be best managed, for the good and prosperity of all.[5]

TRANSCENDENTALISTS AND ABOLITIONISTS

In some respects the heirs of the Antifederalist libertarian legacy were the Transcendentalists and the abolitionists of the pre–Civil War era. Yet their critical perspectives on the Constitution and the republican tradition are replete with ironies. For one thing, the Transcendentalists saw the threat to individual liberty coming not from the Constitution but from the very source that Patrick Henry and others had assumed would save government from its inevitable corruptors and abuses—society. Against the pressures of social conformity, Ralph Waldo Emerson and Henry David Thoreau extolled the values of independence and solitude; and they ridiculed the idea of political virtue, describing it as a kind of social gesture born of pride or guilt. Virtue may be necessary for the preservation of liberty, but they did not believe that politics made virtuous citizens. "Their virtues are penances," Emerson observed of citizens of good works, adding: "I do not wish to expiate, but to live."[6]

In their various essays, particularly "Politics," "Civil Disobedi-ence," and "The Future of the Republic," Emerson and Thoreau made it clear that the Constitution and the government it sus-tained had done little to elevate the people, further the spirit of freedom, settle the West, or inspire the intellect. Emerson's very first credo, his now-famous essay on "Nature" (1836), is generally regarded as the opening proclamation of Transcendentalism in the language of the sublime. Yet the first sentence is less mystical than political, for Emerson has Daniel Webster's ancestor worship of the Founders in mind when he begins: "Our age is retrospec-tive. It builds the sepulchres of the fathers." Webster would become the embodiment of all that Emerson and Thoreau de-spised about American politics when he made his Seventh of March speech supporting the Compromise of 1850. Webster was a "man who lives by memory; a man of the past, not a man of faith and hope. All the drops of his blood have eyes that look downward, and his finely developed understanding only works truly and with all its force when it stands for animal good; that is, for property." Emerson had no patience with a statesman who would have the North pledge itself to upholding the fugitive slave law even if it was the last resort to save the Union. "This filthy enactment was made in the nineteenth century, by people who could read or write. I will not obey it, by God." A Constitu-tion that defended slavery violated the dictates of conscience, and as a result a document designed to preserve republican liberty had allowed its own language to become a monstrous perversion. "The word *liberty* in the mouth of Mr. Webster sounds like the word *love* in the mouth of a courtesan."[7]

Emerson was every bit as concerned with the problem of power as were the Founders, but to him the phenomenon of power as force and might would resolve itself only when people ceased to fear their own restless selves. He and Thoreau recognized that the Founders had devised the Constitution because they did not ex-pect men to be virtuous and master their selfish desires. Hence politics, instead of nurturing civic ideals, would remain simply a matter of "cunning," a shrewd scramble for power and interests. Thus Emerson and Thoreau, two of the most radiant intellects of the nineteenth century, could not return to the republic's "first principles." The "men of '87," Thoreau protested, cannot teach us what must be done. In the case of slavery especially, "the state has provided no way; its very Constitution is the evil."[8]

Many abolitionists agreed with Emerson and Thoreau's critique of politics and their condemnation of the Constitution. Abraham Lincoln was no abolitionist, but even though he had profound disagreements with William Lloyd Garrison over the pace of social change and the tactics of immediate emancipation, both were in agreement on two issues: (1) to the extent that the Constitution protected slavery it violated both the Declaration of Independence and the Christian covenant, and thus (2), slavery had all but destroyed the moral significance of republicanism. Our "republican robe is soiled" by the "sin" of slavery, declared Lincoln. "We prate of integrity, and virtue, and independence, who sell our birthright for office," shouted Garrison in protest of politics as usual. "Is it republicanism to say, that the majority can do no wrong? Then I am not a republican. Is it aristocracy to say, that the people sometimes shamefully abuse their high trust? Then I am an aristocrat."[9]

LINCOLN AND THE CRISIS OF THE UNION

Whatever remained of classical republicanism in American political culture could scarcely survive the Civil War crisis. To appreciate the irrelevance of classical politics three issues can be examined: (1) the allegation, made by both the Republican and Democratic parties, of the existence of a political conspiracy; (2) Lincoln's "house divided" metaphor, a significant departure from the Framers' reasoning and a substitution of biblical moralism for Machiavellian realism; and (3) the Lincoln–Douglas debates, which required that America be defined once and for all by returning to the republic's original principles.

The classical idea that liberty is always threatened by conspiratorial power had haunted English opposition thought in the seventeenth and eighteenth centuries. Bernard Bailyn has shown how the colonists drew upon this paranoid ideology in the 1760s to argue that George III and his parliamentary conspirators were plotting to suppress the liberties of Americans through such measures as the Stamp Act. In the series of crises leading to the Civil War, seemingly similar accusations were hurled by both North

ABRAHAM LINCOLN
Lincoln was committed to the ideals
of the Declaration of Independence,
yet he was ambivalent about the
Constitution and any attempt to return
the nation to "first principles."
(Courtesy of the Library of Congress)

and South. The Republicans carried on the abolitionists' conviction that the "Slave Power" was scheming to reopen the African slave trade as the first step toward the larger design of spreading slavery throughout the West. Seeing history operating behind the scenes, several Republicans even believed that Southerners ultimately wanted to establish slavery in the northern states and thereby deny the civil liberties and labor rights of white as well as black Americans. Conversely, Southerners saw the Republican party as the political arm of the abolitionists who would stop at nothing to emancipate the slaves even if it meant violating the Constitution and forcing the South to secede from the Union. Both sides viewed each other as scheming to subvert the republic, and exponents of each side saw liberty as threatened by tyranny, whether it be of the many or of the few. In the midst of the Civil War, Lincoln felt the need to expose the cant about "liberty" and to show the world what actually was at stake:

> The world has never had a good definition of the word liberty, and the American people, just now, are much in want of one. We all declare for liberty; but in using the same word we do not all mean the same thing. With some the word liberty may mean for his labor; while with others the same word may mean for some men to do as they please with other men, and the product of other men's labor. Here are two, not only different, but incompatible things, called by the same name—liberty. And it follows that each of the things is, by the respective parties, called by two different and incompatible names—liberty and tyranny.
>
> The shepherd drives the wolf from the sheep's throat, for which the sheep thanks the shepherd as a liberator, while the wolf denounces him for the same act as the destroyer of liberty, especially as the sheep was a black one. Plainly the sheep and the wolf are not agreed upon a definition of the word liberty; and precisely the same difference prevails today among us human creatures, even in the North, and all professing to love liberty.[10]

The differing views of liberty and of the forces threatening it mark a significant break with classical traditions. Liberty now had less to do with political independence than with free labor and its rewards, a principle that stood threatened by the contrary idea of liberty that defended human bondage under the right of property. Moreover, classical republicanism rested on the assumption that people had the responsibility to resist encroachments of executive power, and the responsibility for upholding liberty could best be met by locating sovereignty in the legislative branch of government as the embodiment of the popular will. But the slavery issue sectionalized politics far beyond the branches of government. The historian Richard Hildreth, who lived through the Civil War crisis, realized that the older categories of classical thought no longer obtained. It was sectionalism and the doctrine of state's rights, and not the traditional antagonism of the legislative and executive branch and the ministerial conspiracy agitating the Whig mentality, that plagued the Union. "He had the sagacity to perceive what subsequent experience had abundantly confirmed," Hildreth wrote of Alexander Hamilton after the Civil War, "that the Union had rather dread the resistance of the states to federal power than executive usurpation."[11]

The sectional crisis also obscured classical republicanism in other respects. For one thing, the crisis alienated Lincoln from the Founders of the very republic he was determined to preserve. Again and again Lincoln chided the Framers for not condemning or even mentioning slavery in the Constitution, and, after the Dred Scott decision in 1857, he had to confront a new problem: the power to allow or prohibit slavery in the territories now lay with the Supreme Court and not with Congress and the state legislators or territorial conventions, the representative assemblies in which republicanism had located the true source of sovereign authority. Congress, once regarded as the bastion of liberty, could not interfere with the property rights of slaveholders. In this situation Lincoln had no choice but to question the handiwork of 1787 by opening up the issue of racial slavery. Lincoln's "house divided" speech, delivered on June 16, 1858, is starkly apocalyptic. " 'A House divided against itself cannot stand,' " Lincoln declared. "I believe this government cannot endure permanently half slave and half free. I do not expect the house to fall—but I do expect it will cease to be divided. It will become all one thing, or all the other. Either the opponents of slavery will arrest the further spread of it, and place it where the public mind shall rest in the belief that it is in the course of ultimate extinction, or its advocates will push it forward till it shall become alike lawful in all the States—old as well as new, North as well as South."[12]

The curious feature of this passage is the way it departs from the Framers's own intentions and purposes. Lincoln well knew that the Northwest Ordinance had prohibited slavery where it did not exist while the Constitution had tolerated it where it did exist. But in the "house divided" speech he claimed that the compromise of 1787 could not last permanently. It should be recalled that, even aside from slavery, the *Federalist* authors believed that a republic could be divided against itself over such classical antagonisms as "factions" and still be made to endure through institutional safeguards. The expression "A House divided against itself cannot stand" is from scripture, not from "the Science of Politics" enunciated in 1787. Indeed, it was Southern intellectuals who drew upon authors of classical antiquity in an effort to demonstrate the historical compatibility of slavery and republicanism. In order to demonstrate the opposite lesson Lincoln appealed to precisely that which Machiavelli tried to purge from classical realpolitik—the language of moral passion and the conscience of Christianity.

It was in the Lincoln–Douglas debates that the very meaning of the American republic had to be established. Both Lincoln and Senator Douglas opposed the Dred Scott decision and each believed the country must be restored to its commitment to republican freedom. But while Lincoln insisted that slavery and freedom threatened America with a cataclysmic time bomb, Douglas insisted that the nation had been founded on sectional differences about slavery and could continue only by leaving that compromise intact. Lincoln, in turn, claimed that the compromise continued to violate the spirit of '76. "There is no reason in the world why the Negro is not entitled to all the natural rights enumerated in the Declaration of Independence, the right to life, liberty, and the pursuit of happiness [Loud cheers.]"[13] Douglas took the position that the people themselves, in their sovereign capacity to form new states from existing territories, had the right to determine whether their own respective state would be slave or free. Ultimately the debate boiled down to two definitions of the Republic's original foundation—political equality or popular sovereignty.

Neither Lincoln nor Douglas could comfortably invoke the *Federalist* authors, who had made it clear that "the machinery of government" had to control, not realize, both political equality and popular sovereignty. In the end America would find its definition in the authority that comes from the barrel of a gun and the mouth of a cannon on the bloody field of battle. Lincoln's devotion to the Declaration prevailed in the Thirteenth, Fourteenth, and Fifteenth amendments, which made privileges and immunities and the natural rights of due process and equal protection of the laws part of the federal Constitution. But the Civil Rights amendments pushed classical republicanism even further into the background of America's political culture. With power transferred to the federal government and the nation rather than the states now sovereign, the older classical notion of liberty and virtue being promoted at the level of local self-government became more remote than ever. Moreover, when citizenship is finally defined in the Fourteenth Amendment, it is simply a matter of birthplace and naturalization, with no mention that the people had to meet the requirements of classical republicanism. Americans need not prove their dedication to the public good by involving themselves in politics as a test of their capacity for civic virtue. Citizenship is a right, not a duty.

HENRY ADAMS, THEODORE ROOSEVELT, WOODROW WILSON

The Constitution survived the Civil War crisis. But "the machine that would go of itself," as James Russell Lowell described the document, continued to fail to command the esteem of intellectuals after the war just as it had failed to do so before.[14] During the Centennial of 1887, for example, few American writers, scholars, or even historians bothered to show up to celebrate the event in Philadelphia. One American who saw little to celebrate was Henry Adams, the great-grandson of John Adams and one of the nation's greatest historians. More than any American thinker, the young Adams carried in his genes the whole moral lifeblood of classical politics. In *The Education of Henry Adams* he reiterated the ancient conviction that the ultimate purpose of acquiring a political education is "to control power in some form." When investigating the corruption of American politics in the Grant era, he followed the classical tradition and undertook "a recurrence of the fundamental principles of the Constitution" in the hope of finding an answer to the problem of power. But he would conclude that "the moral law had expired—like the Constitution," convinced that "the system of 1789 had broken down, and with it the eighteenth-century fabric of a priori, or moral, principle." Although the Humean-influenced Constitution may not have necessarily depended upon either moral principle or natural law, as Adams assumed, it did rest on a set of assumptions about mixed government and checks and balances that promised to control power. Henry Adams concluded that new forms of corporate power had eluded the mechanisms the Framers had devised. He judged the Constitution's premises "delusive" and "chimerical" because the political authority of the American state proved impotent to discipline the economic power of business interests. And in the absence of political sovereignty, capitalism worked through bribery, patronage, lobbies, rings, party bosses, and political machines to achieve its illicit ends.[15]

Thus like Max Weber, the German social philosopher who visited the United States in the early years of the Progressive era, Adams saw that in America the political system had been penetrated from without by business and corrupted from within by bosses; that, in short, there could be no classical distinction between the political and economic spheres because the party boss himself was a "capitalist" who simply bought and sold votes. And Adams could also agree with Weber that politics and ethics were incompatible realms of value and that the sensitive intellectual should shun "politics as a vocation."[16] Haunted by the nightmares that afflicted English Whig statesmen in the eighteenth century, Adams saw bribery and influence peddling everywhere, the action of government by party bosses working for the creatures of capitalism. "Education could go no further. Tammany Hall stood at the end of the Vista." Adams and Weber shared a conviction that, as we shall see, the Progressive reformer Theodore Roosevelt refused to concede: the union of corporate capitalism and political machines would forever frustrate republican ideals and undermine the spirit of the Constitution. To the anguished Adams, politics itself, once conceived as a noble profession, had lost all sense of shame. "Politics have ceased to interest me," he wrote to Henry Cabot Lodge. "I am satisfied that the machine can't be smashed this time. As I feared, we have ourselves saved it by a foolish attempt to run it, which we shall never succeed in. The caucus and the machine will outlive me. . . . When the day comes on which it will be considered as disgraceful to be seen in a caucus as to be seen in a gambling hall or brothel, then my interest will wake up again and legitimate politics will get a new birth."[17]

That "new birth" would come with the upsurge of Progressivism at the turn of the century. The question that must now be raised is to what extent the Progressive politicians like Theodore Roosevelt and Woodrow Wilson could address the problems whose answers had eluded Henry Adams.

When President Roosevelt went to Paris to deliver an address on "Citizenship in a Republic" at the Sorbonne in 1905, he did not dwell on the penetration of politics by business. Nor did he appear to be concerned about the ethical dilemmas inherent in the nature of politics that had troubled the sensitive minds of Adams and Weber. What did trouble the more robust Roosevelt was the recognition that America's historical development differed from that of Europe. Instead of contending with the kings and tyrants of the Old World, America had to struggle against the "primeval conditions" of the environment; and to the extent that the frontier heritage had shaped the American character, liberal individualism became both the essential principle of American history and its essential problem. "The conditions accentuate vices and virtues, energy and ruthlessness, all the good qualities and all the defects of intense individualism, self-reliant, self-centered, far more conscious of its rights than of its duties, and blind to its own shortcomings. To the hard materialism of the frontier days succeeds the hard materialism of an industrialism even more intense and absorbing than that of older nations."[18]

Roosevelt's answer to the debilities of liberal individualism came to be known as the "New Nationalism," a political state that would render industrial capitalism subservient to the public good. But to regenerate the American republic by political means also required that citizens participate in public affairs, even if this meant that they must become involved in machine politics and associate with party bosses. Unlike Weber, Roosevelt did not see modern politics as structurally fated to thwart the fulfillment of political ideals. On the contrary, Roosevelt called upon Americans to immerse themselves in the rough-and-tumble of local politics, the seamy world of saloon keepers, aldermen, ward heelers, and other fixers and brokers. "Our more intellectual men," Roosevelt complained, "often shrink from the raw coarseness and the eager struggle of political life as if they were women," as if, that is, refinement and delicacy were tantamount to virtue and duty. If politics is left to the low and vulgar, the lesson is clear. "No republic can last if corruption is allowed to eat into its public life. No republic can last if the private citizens sit supinely by and either encourage or tolerate corruption among their representatives." Political activity was not only essential to preventing corruption, but it would also help the processes of socialization. Even machine politics functioned in ways that enabled the helpless individual to enjoy the power and identity that comes from organized activity; and the mutual welfare benefits and employment opportunities that derived from boss-led machines met the needs of immigrants and other marginal Americans.[19]

Above all, participatory citizenship would assure that the American republic could avoid the curse that had undermined republics throughout history—class conflict. All republics in the past, Roosevelt informed his Sorbonne audience, fell because their parties divided along class lines, and it made no difference whether their collapse was due to the rule of a wealthy oligarchy or that of an impoverished mob. Class loyalties not only weakened people's allegiance to their republic, but they also concealed the real emotional basis of political resentments. "Remember always that the same measure of condemnation should be extended to the arrogance which would look down upon or crush any man because he is poor and to the envy and hatred which would destroy a man because he is wealthy." Whatever threatened the public good—civic apathy, class antagonism, race hatred, corporate power, acquisitive individualism—threatened the future of the American republic. Thus Roosevelt, anxious to prevent both class exploitation from above and class plunder from below, preached the republican ideals of civic activity, public duty, and even "disinterestedness" and "sacrifice." He extolled the soldierly qualities of George Washington and the "noble ideals" of Abraham Lincoln. He even called for a return to what he regarded as the original ideals and values of the Founders. "We can keep this Republic true to the principles of those who founded, and of those who afterward preserved it, we can keep it a Republic at all, only by remembering that we must live up to the theory of its founders, to the theory of treating each man on his worth as a man; neither holding it for nor against him that he occupies any particular station in life, so long as he does his duty fairly and well by his fellows and by the nation as a whole."[20]

In an address titled "The College Graduate and Public Life," Roosevelt advised students to read *The Federalist,* "the greatest book of its kind that has ever been written." Ironically, students who had read the book, students like Herbert Croly and Walter Lippmann, who would later become the leading intellectuals of the Progressive era, saw in Madison's grasp of "factions" the very phenomenon that would frustrate republican ideals. But Roosevelt was convinced that the Constitution was "a nearly perfect instrument," and he believed that Americans could take pride in *The Federalist*'s authors for succeeding in doing what the Greek and Roman republics had failed to do: devising a scheme that enabled the political state to expand its territory while at the same time preserving both national unity and local, individual freedom.[21] The deeper issue, however, is whether the American republic as conceived in *The Federalist* was capable of preserving and fostering the essential principle of classical politics—virtue.

On this issue Roosevelt seems entirely within the republican tradition in seeing virtue as being threatened by commerce. Unlike Alexander Hamilton, who believed that unregulated commerce would release bellicose passions sufficient to bring on rivalry and war itself—and unlike Jefferson and Alexis de Tocqueville, who assumed that in America commerce reflected a healthy entrepreneurial energy that would strengthen rather than endanger liberty—Roosevelt remained convinced that commerce unmans the will to fight and conquer. "A peaceful and commercial civilization is always in danger of suffering the loss of virile fighting qualities without which no nation, however cultured, however refined, however thrifty and prosperous, can ever amount to anything." To Roosevelt the comforts of commerce must give way to the challenge of courage, physical as well as moral. "The only man who is more contemptible than the blusterer and bully is the coward. No man is worth much to the commonwealth if he is not capable of feeling righteous wrath and just indignation, if he is not stirred to anger by misdoing, and is not impelled to see justice meted out to the wrongdoers." To the modern vices of sloth and ease, Roosevelt juxtaposed "the strenuous life" of heroic effort, a Spartan demand that the citizen dedicate himself to fulfilling four overriding imperatives: the republican imperative of involving oneself in the political life of the nation; the martial imperative of cultivating the "great virile virtues" so as to be willing to take up arms in defense of the nation's honor; the Protestant imperative of hard work and productive effort that will benefit the nation; and the biological imperative of procreating in order that the nation "shall leave its seed to inherit the land." Curiously, Roosevelt esteemed the latter imperative as the most basic of all. "It was the crown of blessings in Biblical times. . . . The greatest of all curses is the curse of sterility, and the severest of all condemnations should be that visited upon wilful sterility."[22] In Roosevelt's version of republicanism virtue is identified with virility and liberty is threatened by impotence.

It seems strange that a president of the United States felt it necessary to tell young French students that sex is more a political duty than a pleasurable delight. But virility had also been one of Machiavelli's favorite virtues, and perhaps he too would agree that a republic depends upon citizens who not only have the courage to fight but the desire to beget. Roosevelt offered America a martial, lusty republicanism that may have struck emotions touched by an episode like the Spanish–American War. With the coming of World War I, however, the American people received a different message from President Woodrow Wilson. Now the purpose of politics was to make the world safe for commerce.

Wilson and Roosevelt both saw themselves as "Progressive" presidents determined to reform the Republic, but their meditations on political philosophy differed in several respects—and not only because Wilson represented the cloistered academic type that Roosevelt disdained. Wilson was also more critical of the machine politics that Roosevelt viewed as legitimate, and he wanted to see America adopt the British cabinet system of government that Roosevelt found "entirely incompatible with our governmental institutions."[23] Perhaps more significantly, Wilson was considerably less enamored of the Founders and some of the specific forms of government they bequeathed to the nation, and he was not altogether sure that the American people could return to the Republic's "first principles" without first reexamining them. No less than Roosevelt did Wilson aspire to regenerate the Republic, and he would look to Abraham Lincoln to show the way. But in

Lincoln, Wilson perceived within the body politic of republican-ism the deeper soul of American liberalism.

"A great man, but, in my judgment, not a great American."[24] Thus spoke Wilson of Alexander Hamilton, whose elitist proclivi-ties supposedly put him out of touch with America's democratic realities. Wilson criticized other of the early statesmen as well. Though a Jeffersonian himself in some respects, Wilson felt that Jefferson had allowed French ideas to distort his thinking; and Madison, like Hamilton, had tried to apply English models to American conditions. John Adams and John C. Calhoun were rejected as simply "great provincials." Wilson felt more sympathy for Washington, Patrick Henry, Benjamin Franklin, and Andrew Jackson, all of whom were closer to the "canons of Americanism," which he defined, in thoughts similar to Tocqueville's and Freder-ick Jackson Turner's, as a new "spirit" that had little to do with European traditions.

> The American spirit is something more than the old, the imme-morial Saxon spirit of liberty from which it sprung. It has been bred by the conditions attending the great task which we have all the century been carrying forward: the task, at once material and ideal, of subduing a wilderness and covering all the wide stretches of a vast continent with a single free and stable polity. It is, accordingly, above all things, a hopeful and confident spirit. It is progressive, optimistically progressive, and ambitious of objects of national scope and advantage.[25]

Given his optimistic views of progress, it is curious that Wil-son admired most Abraham Lincoln, whose Calvinist visions of sin and damnation made American liberalism more a moral bur-den than a political blessing. But in Turnerian terms Wilson explained why Lincoln must be judged "the supreme American of our history," whose mind and temperament summed up the na-tion's character: "The rude Western strength, tempered with shrewdness and a broad human wit; the Eastern conservatism, regardful of law and devoted to strict standards of duty. . . . To the Eastern politicians he seemed like an accident; but to history he must seem like a providence."[26] Wilson had also been influ-enced by several English political philosophers, namely Walter Bagehot, John Bright, and Richard Cobden. But his essay on

Edmund Burke reveals his liberal bourgeois sympathy for the "laborious life" of the philosopher–legislator as opposed to the "idle years" of Burke's rival, the Duke of Bedford. Wilson praised the "splendid pride" of the "formidable Celt" who rose from obscurity to develop a political philosophy that would save aristocracies from their own vices. In Burke, Wilson found a marvelous synthesis of the classical principle of duty and the liberal principle of ambition.[27]

Yet what frustrated duty and ambition in America was the nature of the political system itself. In *Congressional Government* (1884) Wilson described how a weak president stood helplessly by as power and authority slipped from his office into the labyrinth of the legislature's standing committees—the bureaucratization of government that Weber would later analyze. But it was not only the way in which American government developed that troubled Wilson. A government that had been originally conceived to function on the basis of counterpoise merely created unnecessary rivalry among its branches and fragmented the meaning of sovereign authority. In a later book, *Constitutional Government in the United States* (1908), he questioned whether diversity was sufficient to sustain liberty, as Madison had assumed. "You cannot compound a successful government out of antagonisms." Nor can it evolve from committee structures. The ancient Roman assembly, Wilson observed, avoided such an impasse because Roman laws could not be amended in their passage and hence "a clearness and technical perfection" characterized their legislative process.[28] Should the American republic, then, return to the classical traditions of antiquity or even to its own "first principles" enunciated in the eighteenth century?

Unlike Roosevelt, Wilson seemed to be more aware of the difficulties involved in such a *ricorso*. For one thing, the classical political tradition had asserted the authority of a parliament against the executive branch on the assumption that the people displayed their civic virtue in resisting monarchical power and ministerial corruption. Such a tradition offered little guidance on how the legislative branch of government, now the source of lobbies and other corrupting influences, could reform itself by enhancing the authority of the executive. Nor did *The Federalist* devote much attention to the office of the presidency. Moreover, to which "first principles" would Americans return, those of 1776 or those of 1787? In contrast to Lincoln, Wilson did not regard the Declaration of Independence as the "sheet anchor" of the Republic, the original covenant that Americans are obligated to uphold. The generation that wrote and read the Declaration may have felt their "bosoms swell against George III," Wilson noted, but the document "did not mention the questions of our day." A further problem was that the Progressives' demand for the referendum, initiative, recall, and the direct election of senators, which Wilson supported, may have represented a break from the theories of *The Federalist*'s authors, who believed that a republic is best preserved to the extent that the people are distanced from the government. Wilson may have occasionally referred to the era of the Founders as the "heroic age," but the essential message of Machiavelli's *ridurre ai principii* becomes problematic in American Progressive thought.[29]

Although Wilson, a learned scholar of western political thought, defended Machiavelli's controversial reputation and his "exalted" aim of fusing liberty and order, he did not see history as characterized by the Aristotelian cycle of freedom and tyranny.[30] Nor did he believe that America could return to the Republic's "first principles." In a series of essays that appeared in 1913 as "The New Freedom," Wilson took a close look at the theoretical presuppositions of *The Federalist*'s authors. The problem with the Constitution was the "Newtonian theory" which formed its foundations and led the Framers to believe that government could be constructed like a "solar system" of predictable laws of action and reaction. "The makers of our Federal Constitution read Montesquieu with true scientific enthusiasm. . . . And they constructed a government as they would have constructed an orrery,—to display the laws of nature." Wilson wanted to see a government based on the principles of growth and adaptation, a government "accountable to Darwin, not to Newton." He did not seem to fear, as did Weber, that a government based upon the principles of organic growth would lead to higher forms of development resulting in the atrophy of bureaucratization and specialization. "Government is not a body of blind forces; it is a body of men, with highly differentiated functions, no doubt, in our modern day, of specialization. . . . There can be no successful government without the intimate, instinctive coordination of the organs of life and action. . . .

Living political constitutions must be Darwinian in structure and practice. Society is a living organism and must obey the laws of life, not of mechanics; it must develop."[31]

Here Wilson departs emphatically from the classical tradition of politics. In that honored tradition the state, rather than reflecting the "laws of life," is to exercise its authority over the unruliness of "natural" society. Here, too, we encounter a curious twist in the fate of republican thought. In contrast to Roosevelt, Wilson saw machine politics, patronage, and other aspects of political corruption as not only threatening the Republic but jeopardizing the very meaning of freedom—and freedom he conceived not in the classical sense of civic participation but in the "purer" sense of commercial action. Thus Wilson saw his "New Freedom" as breaking apart the politico-business alliance that had spread like a cancer in corporate America. He wanted above all to create opportunity for "the men who are on the make," the ambitious Americans who only ask the government for "fair play" in the marketplace which, depending upon circumstance, may or may not require state regulation. Wilson looked forward to a time when every American could be an aspiring entrepreneur. "But I feel confident that if Jefferson were living in our day he would see what we see," lamented Wilson as he described monopolies and trusts frustrating innovation and darkening "the liberating light of individual initiative, of individual liberty, of individual freedom, the light of untrammeled enterprise." To a Jeffersonian who believed "in human liberty as I believe in the wine of life," corporate America could only be judged a "tragic failure."[32]

Yet Wilson was a Calvinist as well as a Jeffersonian, and the fusion of these two temperaments created dilemmas for American liberalism and made classical republicanism an even more complicated proposition. Wilson's Calvinist belief in hard work and individual initiative meant that economic life should not only be liberated from political authority but that economics and politics themselves are distinct realms of value. In his political philosophy, as we have seen, Wilson deplored rivalry among congressional committees, lack of coordination in the branches of government, and the antagonisms of an electorate that thwarted national unity and purpose. In his economic philosophy, however, he extolled self-reliance, ambition, and unhampered individual liberty. For the sake of good government, political man is to be cooperative; but if America is ever to aspire to the "New Freedom," economic man must be competitive. "No living thing," Wilson had written in reference to the counterpoised mechanisms of the Constitution, "can have its organs offset against each other, as checks, and live."[33] In the economic race of life, however, the "men who are on the make" are to offset themselves against each other as the very definition of liberty. Thus ambition, self-interest, and commerce—the very elements that were once seen as threatening republican virtue—become in Wilson's thinking the elements that would liberate America from the coming of corporate power.

Whatever the successes or failures of the "New Freedom," Wilson was the last president not only to write many of his own speeches but to think deeply about the meaning of politics and the nature of government in America. Henceforth that task would be taken up by intellectuals and scholars, political observers rather than political participants. But even eminent Progressive intellectuals like Herbert Croly, Walter Lippmann, and Charles Beard had no more success in finding America's "first principles."[34] A concluding comment on the futility of that search is perhaps in order.

The split between the Federalists and Antifederalists suggests the difficulty of returning to the origins of the American Republic in order to establish its meaning. Lincoln and the abolitionists were closer to the Antifederalists in insisting that the nation had its political birth in 1776. The Federalists and subsequent statesmen like Daniel Webster looked to 1787 as the historic moment of the Republic's conception. The split perhaps goes to the heart of America's own ambivalence toward fixed definitions and final meanings. The Declaration of Independence gave the nation a body of egalitarian principles and rights that are "natural" and "unalienable." The Constitution gave the nation a series of articles specifying how government is to be organized and political authority divided. The ringing certitudes of the Declaration aimed to restrict the reach of government; the somber provisions of the Constitution aimed to augment its "sphere." One document proclaims the grounds on which Americans are entitled to regard themselves as free; the other provides the rules that legitimates the actions of government. It could be said that while the Declaration aims to advance liberty, the Constitution aims to control power. There may be no conflict between these two political objectives. But precisely because the author of the Declaration denied that the past should bind the present and the authors of the Constitution defined the new Republic as an "experiment," the Founders themselves acknowledged there would be no clear, unambiguous "first principles" to which Americans must return. Even Lincoln, despite his devotion to the Declaration, was convinced that "we cannot look backwards for guidance." "The dogmas of the quiet past are inadequate to the stormy present," he told Congress in 1862. "The occasion is piled high with difficulty, and we must rise with the occasion. As our case is new, so we must think anew, and act anew. We must disenthrall ourselves, and then we shall save our country."[35]

Notes

1. Joseph Agresto, " 'A System without Precedent'—James Madison and the Revolution in Republican Liberty," *South Atlantic Quarterly* 82 (Spring 1983): 129–44.

2. Patrick Henry's speech to the Virginia convention is reprinted in *The Antifederalists*, ed. Cecelia M. Kenyon (Indianapolis: Bobbs-Merrill, 1966), 238–64.

3. *Federalist* Nos. 1, 9, 10, 27, 51.

4. Isaiah Berlin, *Four Essays on Liberty* (New York: Oxford University Press, 1969), 118–72.

5. Joyce Appleby, *Capitalism and the New Social Order?* (New York: New York University Press, 1984); Jefferson's ideas on "ward democracy" are examined in Garrett Ward Sheldon, *The Political Philosophy of Thomas Jefferson* (forthcoming, Pennsylvania State University Press); and Hannah Arendt, *On Revolution* (New York: Viking Press, 1963), 252–59. For a critique of Arendt's neoclassical interpretation, see my "Death of Democracy? Charles A. Beard, Hannah Arendt, and the Constitution," *University of Chicago Law Thesaurus* (forthcoming). Jefferson's warning that wards are essential to prevent directions from Washington is in his *Autobiography*, in *The Writings of Thomas Jefferson*, 20 vols. (1853; reprint, Washington, D.C., 1907 [c 1905]), 1:82.

6. Ralph Waldo Emerson, "Self-Reliance," in *Ralph Waldo Emerson: Selected Prose and Poetry*, ed. Reginald L. Cook (New York: Rinehart and Co., 1950), 170.

7. Emerson, "Nature," in ibid., 3–46; Emerson's diatribes against Webster are quoted from the excellent essay by Harold Bloom, "Mr. America," *New York Review of Books* (November 22, 1984), 19–24.

8. Henry David Thoreau, "Civil Disobedience," in *Walden and Other Essays*, ed. Joseph Wood Krutch (New York: Bantam Books, 1962), 85–104.

9. William Lloyd Garrison, Fourth of July Address, 1829, reprinted in *William Lloyd Garrison*, ed. George M. Frederickson (Englewood Cliffs, N.J.: Prentice-Hall, 1968), 11.

10. *The Collected Works of Abraham Lincoln*, ed. Roy P. Basler, 8 vols. (New Brunswick, N.J.: Rutgers University Press, 1953), 7:301–2.

11. Hildreth is quoted in Bert James Loewenberg, *American History in American Thought* (New York: Simon and Schuster, 1972), 279.

12. Basler, *Collected Works*, 2:461.

13. Ibid., 3:16.

14. Michel Kammen, *A Machine That Would Go of Itself: The Cultural Impact of the Constitution* (New York: Alfred A. Knopf, 1986).

15. Henry Adams, *The Education of Henry Adams* (New York: The Modern Library, 1931),

3–53; Adams, *The Great Secession Winter of 1860–61 and Other Essays,* ed. George Hoch-field (New York: Sagamore Press, 1958), 1–33, 95–190.

16. Max Weber, "Politics as a Vocation," in *From Max Weber: Essays in Sociology,* ed. Hans Gerth and C. W. Mills (New York: Oxford University Press, 1946).

17. Henry Adams to Henry Cabot Lodge, June 24, 1876, *The Letters of Henry Adams,* ed. J. C. Levenson et al., 3 vols. (Cambridge, Mass.: Harvard Universitry Press, Belknap Press, 1982), 2:279.

18. Theodore Roosevelt, "Citizenship in a Republic," in *The Works of Theodore Roosevelt,* 24 vols. (New York: Charles Scribner's Sons, 1923–26), 15:27–35.

19. "Machine Politics in New York City," "Corruption," in ibid., 76–98, 538.

20. "The Manly Virtues," "Duties of American Citizenship," "Machine Politics," "Citizenship in a Republic," "Cooperation and the Simple Life," in ibid., 27–28, 281–96, 523–24, 531.

21. "The College Graduate and Public Life," in ibid., 36–46.

22. "The Manly Virtues," "Citizenship in a Republic," in ibid., 32, 513–14.

23. "The College Graduate and Public Life," in ibid., 42–43.

24. Woodrow Wilson, "Freemen Need No Guardians," in *The New Freedom,* ed. William E. Leuchtenburg (Englewood Cliffs, N.J.: Prentice-Hall, 1961), 47.

25. Woodrow Wilson, "A Calender of Great Americans," in *Mere Literature and Other Essays* (Boston: Houghton Mifflin, 1896), 199–208.

26. Ibid.

27. Woodrow Wilson, "Edmund Burke and the French Revolution" (1901), reprinted in *The Burke-Paine Controversy,* ed. Ray B. Browne (New York: Harcourt, Brace and World, 1963), 138–44.

28. Woodrow Wilson, *Congressional Government* (1884; reprint, New York: Meridian ed., 1956), 86; *Constitutional Government in the United States* (1908; reprint, New York: Columbia University Press, 1961), 60.

29. Woodrow Wilson, "What Is Progress?" "Liberation of Vital Energies," in *The New Freedom* (New York: Doubleday, Page, 1913), 42, 162.

30. Henry Wilkinson Bragdon, *Woodrow Wilson: The Academic Years* (Cambridge, Mass.: Harvard University Press, Belknap Press, 1967), 255-63. I am indebted to this study of the development of Wilson's early political thought.

31. Wilson, "What Is Progress?" 41–42.

32. Wilson, "Liberation of Vital Energies," 164–65.

33. Wilson, "What Is Progress?" 41–42.

34. John P. Diggins, "Progressivism and Republicanism," *American Quarterly* 37 (1985): 572–98.

35. Basler, *Collected Works,* 5:537.

S ome of the best recent writing on Revolutionary America has been done by legal scholars. They have emphasized the complexity of constitutional issues debated in that era, and they have shown the central role that debate played in the coming of the American Revolution as well as in forming the new United States. Thomas C. Grey made his contribution to this growing body of literature in a series of essays published in the *Stanford Law Review*. A professor of law at Stanford University, Grey attended Stanford as an undergraduate, receiving his A.B. in 1963. He went on as a Marshall scholar to take a B.A. at Brasenose College, Oxford University; he then earned his LL.B. at Yale University in 1968.

In his earlier essays Professor Grey traced the American attachment to and understanding of fundamental law, and he returns to that subject here. Americans of the Revolutionary era, he observes, inherited as part of the English legal tradition belief in a higher law that could not be struck down by statute. The unwritten English constitution—a combination of common law traditions, key documents like Magna Carta, and natural law as well as statutes passed by Parliament—was venerated by some jurists as inviolable. Many leading Americans felt likewise, and the War of Independence and need to create governments changed their circumstances more than their thought. The Founders, therefore, apparently believed that there was a fundamental law to which they were answerable, an unwritten constitution that supplements the document they drafted in 1787. Nonetheless, Grey advises, we tread on shaky ground when we try to define the limits of that unwritten constitution or attempt to determine what is constitutionally appropriate for our own age by adverting to the Founders' "intent." As Professor Grey warned in one of his law review articles, there is a danger in giving the Constitution the power of scripture, or in granting the judges who interpret it the voice of prophets.

VI

THE ORIGINAL UNDERSTANDING AND THE UNWRITTEN CONSTITUTION

★

Thomas C. Grey

The doctrine of *Marbury v. Madison* has long been settled in American constitutional law; judges are to enforce the clear commands of our written constitutions against contrary legislation. There is no comparable consensus on the question of whether we have a supplementary, judicially enforceable unwritten constitution as well.[1] After engaging constitutional theorists almost to the point of exhaustion for more than a decade, debate on this question has recently flared up again, in the spectacularly public Bicentennial contest over the nomination of Judge Bork to the Supreme Court.

Here I venture some observations on how the question of the unwritten constitution was understood in the Founding period. These observations have only limited application to the present debate. The phoenix-like American unwritten constitution had a second "origin" in the period of Reconstruction; on this issue as on others, we must take account of the possibility that "the Union survived the Civil War, but the Constitution did not."[2] Nor, in any event, do I think that original understanding can settle what we should be doing now. But with a living constitution as with a human being, it is natural to take an interest in the circumstances of birth.[3]

One way to begin an inquiry into how the Framers regarded the question of the unwritten constitution is to see what they said about it in the written one. This directs our attention to the Ninth Amendment: "The enumeration in the Constitution, of certain rights, shall not be construed to deny or disparage others retained by the people." It is natural to read these words as implying acceptance of an unwritten constitution, made up of unenumerated rights that are conceived as having the full force of fundamental law. And yet alternative interpretations are possible. Perhaps the unenumerated rights were not conceived as part of constitutional law—perhaps they were only thought of as natural or moral or political rights, not to be enforced as such by courts against contrary legislation otherwise valid. Or perhaps the "other" rights referred to were those that had been expressly enumerated in state constitutions but not in the federal Bill of Rights; on this interpretation, the Ninth Amendment was inserted only as a precaution against inferring any negative implications from this omission for the operation of these rights as a matter of state law.[4]

The availability of a range of plausible conflicting readings suggests that, as usual, perusal of the text by itself cannot reveal what it meant to those who adopted it. The inquiry must look outward and backward, to the surrounding and preceding context of thought and practice.

CHASE AND IREDELL

As we start to look into this broader context, we find at least one clear indication that the question of the judicial enforceability of an unwritten constitution was a live issue during the early national period. Supreme Court Justices Samuel Chase and James Iredell debated that very question in *Calder v. Bull* in 1798.[5] The precise issue in the case was whether the Connecticut legislature could constitutionally intervene in the course of private litigation, something colonial assemblies and early state legislatures had frequently done with a fine disregard for Montesquieuan proprieties.[6] Calder claimed a piece of land that had been left to Bull in a disputed will. The probate court found the will invalid;

but the legislature ordered a judicial rehearing, and this time the will was upheld. Calder appealed that judgment to the U.S. Supreme Court, claiming that the legislative intervention was an unconstitutional ex post facto law.

The Court unanimously rejected the appeal, with Justice Chase writing the lead opinion. Chase relied mainly on arguments from text and history to conclude that the federal ex post facto clause prohibited only retroactive criminal penalties. But to the conventional legal argument he added a practical observation: while retroactive criminal laws were invariably unjust, retroactive civil statutes were sometimes fair and occasionally even necessary.[7] On the other hand, he noted, if the clause was read narrowly to apply only to criminal law, this would leave some crude state legislative abuses outside its scope—including that standard nightmare of respectable lawyers, "a law that takes property from A and gives it to B."[8]

Indeed, the facts of *Calder* suggested that it might involve just such a law: the courts had decided a property dispute in one party's favor, and a legislative intervention had caused the property to end up with the other party. But Chase found reasons to conclude that the Connecticut legislature had not simply decreed an arbitrary transfer from the worthy Calder to the undeserving Bull. First, the legislative grant of a rehearing had left the final determination of the case to the regular courts; and, second, the original probate decision had only created an expectancy or *in personam* "right to recover property" in Calder, but had fallen short of actually vesting him with a full-fledged *in rem* "right to property."[9]

Even if these technicalities were persuasive, there remained the objection that the narrow construction of the ex post facto clause would in other cases leave the fundamental outrage of a legislative transfer of property from A to B without constitutional remedy. Chase's response was that the judiciary had at its disposal a supplemental unwritten constitution which would catch the cases of flagrant injustice that fell through the gaps in the written one:

> I cannot subscribe to the omnipotence of a state legislature, or that it is absolute and without control; although its authority should not be expressly restrained by the constitution. . . .
> There are certain vital principles in our free Republican govern-

ments, which will determine and overrule an apparent and flagrant abuse of legislative powers. . . . An act of the Legislature
(*for I cannot call it a law*) contrary to the great first principles of
the social compact, cannot be considered a rightful exercise of
legislative authority.[10]

Present-day readers are sometimes confused by Chase's argument. Previously to the passage just quoted, he had affirmed the
understanding, conventional then as it is now, that the states
were governments of general jurisdiction; they had all the "powers of legislation" not "expressly taken away" by the United States
Constitution.[11] At the same time, he seemed to say in the passage
quoted, this plenary legislative power was not so plenary after all.
But how can state legislative power be both unlimited, express
prohibitions aside, and at the same time limited by "certain vital
principles?" Chase resolved the apparent contradiction through
the emphasized phrase "for I cannot call it a law." Republican
legislatures had power to pass all *laws* not prohibited to them, but
not everything going under legislative form—and in particular
not a piece of legislation violating vested rights, for example by
taking A's property and giving it to B—counted as a law. In
common with a long tradition in political discourse, Chase simply presupposed that a republic must be a government under
law—"an empire of laws, and not of men"—and that this requirement was more than a purely formal one.[12]

Chase's blend of individual rights and separation of powers
claims would become a standard move in nineteenth-century constitutional argument: in 1810, John Marshall would say that "to
the [state] legislature is granted all legislative power" but doubt
that confiscation of property was "in the nature of legislative
power"; in 1819 Daniel Webster would characterize legislative
violations of vested rights as "rather sentences than laws"; in 1840
a New York court would say that neither the transfer of a piece of
property nor the imprisonment of an individual "can be done by
mere legislation"; and, as the Fourteenth Amendment was being
ratified in 1868, Thomas Cooley would write that a legislature's
taking from A to give to B was either an invalid attempt to
exercise power inherently judicial or "a mere arbitrary fiat."[13]

It is out of this connection of the separation of powers with
notions of "government of laws" or "the Rule of Law" that the

doctrine of substantive due process arises. The root idea is that when legislation effectively operates to deprive persons of liberty or property without grounds normally recognized at common law, the deprivation is not according to "the law of the land" (or "due process" or "due course of law"), even though the legislative decree in question may be processed through ordinary judicial procedures. A statute decreeing transfer of Blackacre from A to B is not saved by provision for a trial in which the only triable issues are the identity of A, B, and Blackacre.[14]

Chase not only anticipated the future; he was also continuing a well-established tradition of constitutional argument when he appealed to unwritten principles as a restraint on legislative power. What marked *Calder* as special was not so much Chase's pronouncement as the response it drew from Justice James Iredell. Iredell gave what seems to have been the first explicit statement of full-fledged constitutional positivism: the doctrine that judicial review can enforce written but not unwritten constitutional principles. He recognized that "some speculative jurists" had said that a law violating natural justice was void but denied that "any Court of Justice would possess a power to declare it so." The "abstract principles of natural justice" provided "no fixed standard," so that a legislature had "an equal right of opinion" on such a question.[15]

THE PRE-REVOLUTIONARY BACKGROUND

Iredell's exclusively positivist conception of constitutional restriction on legislative power ran counter to a tradition well-established long before 1798.[16] The generation of Americans who made the Revolution conducted their whole struggle against Parliament on the basis of what they conceived as a legally binding unwritten constitution—the British constitution, which they understood in terms of Bolingbroke's famous definition (1735) as "that Assemblage of Laws, Institutions and Customs, derived from certain fix'd Principles of Reason, directed to certain fix'd Objects of Publick Good, that compose the general System, according to which the Community hath agreed to be govern'd." As Bolingbroke had also said—and this was the key point for the Americans—the constitution was fixed; "a Parliament cannot annul" it.[17]

The colonists had argued that Parliament's taxes and, as their case evolved, its legislative regulations as well were illegal violations of that constitution. It was to these arguments that John Adams referred when he wrote years later: "What do we mean by the Revolution? The War? That was no part of the Revolution. It was only an Effect and Consequence of it." The true revolution, he said, had been "in the minds of the people, and was effected, from 1760 to 1775" by arguments recorded in "the records of thirteen Legislatures, the Pamphlets, Newspapers" through which "public opinion was enlightened and informed concerning the Authority of Parliament over the Colonies."[18] Elsewhere, Adams dated the beginning of this process more precisely; "the child Independence was born" on that day in 1761 when James Otis challenged the legal validity of the parliamentary authorization for general search warrants, saying, "An act against the constitution is void; an act against natural equity is void: and . . . the executive courts must pass such acts into disuse."[19]

During the whole pre-independence struggle, the American Whigs were to repeat, in one version or another, this invocation of a legally supreme British constitution, compounded of tradition and natural law—against the Sugar Act, the Stamp Act, the Declaratory Act, the use of vice-admiralty courts to try customs violators, the Port of Boston Act, and ultimately against any exercise of parliamentary legislative authority in the colonies. Usually they made explicit that not only justice and policy but constitutional *law* was on their side; the statutes against which they protested were not merely wrong or even "unconstitutional" but, as in Otis's seminal argument, "void" and "illegal." Of course these arguments were not normally made to courts, but to the public in the newspapers, pamphlets, and petitions to which Adams referred—though there were a few instances in which litigation became the vehicle for constitutional protest.

Only at the end, at the moment of independence itself, did the colonists abandon the framework of constitutional argument and invoke pure extralegal natural rights. But the bold revolutionary rhetoric of the Declaration of Independence was very different from the main line of American discourse, which relied largely on English history and law, invoking natural justice only insofar as it was thought to be part of the law and the constitution. The point crucial for understanding the Revolutionary consciousness is that the arguments consistently took constitutional form and used legal language. Of all revolutionaries in history, the American Whigs—even the most radical of them—were perhaps the most legalistic.

The colonists drew their traditions of disputation from seventeenth-century English politics, which likewise involved a revolution ideologically founded on constitutionalism. On the Continent the seventeenth century had seen the rise of absolutist political ideology, couched in the abstract terms of Enlightenment natural law and social contract theory. But English political argument had remained dominated by the medieval assumption that all government was conducted under the control of an overarching, unwritten fundamental law. And the English constitutionalists of the seventeenth century had added to this tradition, as a minor though significant strand, the judicial interpretation and application of fundamental law as an implied limitation on legislative power.

The most famous expression of this view was Sir Edward Coke's statement in *Dr. Bonham's Case* (1610), that "where an Act of Parliament is against common right and reason . . . the common law will control it and adjudge it to be void."[20] Legal commentary and judicial precedent associated "common right and reason" with universal natural law, as well as with that immemorial and nationally specific customary tradition that English lawyers saw as the basis of their common law. Natural law and common law were in turn linked to the ancient unwritten constitution of English government which both sides invoked in a series of important seventeenth-century controversies, in many of which the courts ruled on the constitutionality of Acts of Parliament. Thus Coke wrote in *Calvin's Case* (1609) that the eternal and unchanging law of nature was part of English law and overrode conflicting earthly law.[21] And a royalist lord chief justice wrote, in the *Ship Money Case* (1637), that "Acts of Parliament to take away . . . royal power in defense of the kingdom are void."[22]

The Cokean tradition blended traditional private law, the customary constitution of English government, and the rhetoric of natural law into a conglomerated "fundamental law," which was binding on the legislature and which—so it was said from time to time—judges could enforce. This tradition had begun to lose its force in English law and government after the Revolution of

1688, as the notion of the absolute sovereignty of Parliament gradually took hold. But by the mid-eighteenth century, this transformation was not yet complete in England. The standard practical law books still invoked Coke's great authority for the proposition that the courts would disregard statutes that violated the implied limitations set by "common right and reason"; thus Otis drew his argument in the writs of assistance case from *Viner's Abridgement,* one of the most popular lawyers' digests.[23] And for those who liked their law fancy and up-to-date rather than plain and old-fashioned, Burlamaqui and Vattel, the most influential European legal writers of the period, carried forward the public law tradition of Grotius and Pufendorf, thus reinforcing the prestige of the idea that both natural law and the fundamental law of the constitution were legally binding and supreme over ordinary legislation.

In his *Commentaries* (1765), Blackstone accurately expressed the ideological ambivalence of an English legal profession midway in the transition from the Cokean tradition to the modern positivistic conception of law as the command of a sovereign legislature. He affirmed that the law of nature is "of course superior in obligation to any other. . . . No human laws are of any validity, if contrary to this."[24] At the same time, he stressed what had become a dogma of Enlightenment political theory: that in every government there must be an absolutely sovereign lawgiver. In England this could only be Parliament, and Blackstone lavished some of his choicest rhetoric on the absolute quality of parliamentary sovereignty.[25]

The supremacy of fundamental law clashed with parliamentary sovereignty on the question of judicial review, and here Blackstone resolved his equivocation by giving the priority to legislative supremacy. After noting that it "was generally laid down" that acts of Parliament contrary to reason were void, Blackstone narrowed the *Bonham* doctrine to a canon of statutory construction; judges should treat as void unreasonable "collateral consequences" of a statute. For courts to disregard a statute altogether on grounds of reason or natural justice would "set the judicial power above that of the legislature, which would be subversive of all government."[26]

Blackstone had sensed the movement of English thought; in another generation absolute parliamentary supremacy would be an unchallengeable dogma among English lawyers, and judicial review on the basis of an unwritten fundamental law would be inconceivable. But it is wrong to suppose that even in England the Cokean tradition was dead in the 1760s; Blackstone, after all, did describe the notion of the legal invalidity of legislation violating reason or the constitution as what was "generally laid down." And the old doctrine still had rhetorical force. Parliamentary critics of the government's American policy invoked Coke for the proposition that "an Act of Parliament against common right is a nullity"; and Lord Camden, a former lord chancellor and chief justice, said on the floor of the House of Lords that taxing the unrepresented Americans was "absolutely illegal, contrary to the fundamental laws of nature, contrary to the fundamental laws of this constitution."[27]

In the colonies, the Cokean tradition had maintained more vigor still. There, parliamentary sovereignty was an abstraction, never the daily reality of government it was in England. And Blackstone's authoritative statement of the doctrine had not yet appeared when the disputes over taxation and representation first broke out. The older notion of binding fundamental law thus had both institutional reality and immediate rhetorical appeal for the colonists, which ensured an inhospitable reception for the new doctrine when the *Commentaries* did arrive. Jefferson spoke for many Americans when he contrasted the sound Whig learning of Coke with Blackstone's "honied Mansfieldism."[28] And the central ideological place that the Cokean tradition thereafter played in the Revolutionary struggle gave the idea of a legally binding unwritten constitution compounded of historic tradition and natural reason a high prestige in the minds of the Americans of the Revolutionary generation.

By contrast to the tradition of the unwritten constitution, it was a relatively new idea in 1776 that a written constitution might legally restrain governmental power. Of course, a notion that triumphed so rapidly and dramatically was not born from nothing. Some colonists had experience with constitutive documents of their own; the Mayflower Compact and the Massachusetts Body of Liberties were familiar examples. Some treated the Bible as a source of law, and the Protestant tradition of biblical exegesis influenced their legal thought. Perhaps most important, the colonists had been accustomed to arguing from their colonial

supplant, or did they only supplement, the older notion of a legally binding unwritten constitution compounded of historically rooted tradition and notions of natural justice?

To this question there was in the period following 1776 no conclusive *a priori* answer. On the one hand, American constitutional theory and practice were transformed between independence and the Philadelphia Convention by the emergence of a consensus around the idea of the sovereignty of the people, an idea given institutional form by the convention device. On the other hand, the Cokean constitutional tradition had been at the heart of American revolutionary ideology; when independence came, the idea of the unwritten constitution as fundamental law had the greatest possible prestige and acceptance among Americans. Reflecting this tradition, most of the state constitutions themselves contained open-ended statements of natural rights that echoed the Declaration of Independence. A characteristic provision was Article I of the Massachusetts Declaration of Rights, which provided:

> All men are born free and equal, and have certain natural, essential, and unalienable rights; *among which* may be reckoned the rights of enjoying and defending their lives and liberties; that of acquiring, possessing, and protecting property; in fine, that of seeking their safety and happiness.[36]

Especially among those worried by the spread of measures reflecting supposed "popular licence" within the new states—harassment of loyalists, debtor relief laws, paper money—it was common to invoke the fundamental law–natural rights tradition to urge that there were implied limitations on legislative power in addition to the express ones enacted in the new constitutions. And it was these issues of "democratic excess" that perhaps most agitated the Framers; Madison would say, behind closed doors in Philadelphia, that it was the outbreak of violations of property and contract rights within the states, more even than the external weakness of the Confederation, that provided the strongest motive uniting those who brought the federal convention together.[37]

Given the opposing strands of thought, one might, in support of Iredell, say that the colonists during the period 1761 to 1776 had only been Cokeans *faute de mieux* and were ready to be

Blackstonians now that something better—in the form of their own written constitutions framed in their own conventions—had come along. On the other hand, one could say, in support of Chase—and not only conservatives, but also strong republicans like Jefferson *did* say this—that Americans still believed in an indefinite range of inalienable rights and, as they had distrusted kings and parliaments, they now distrusted majorities as caretakers of these rights.[38] This line of thought supported the Cokean tradition. The outcome of the clash between these possibilities was in fact not a choice of one over the other, but a confusing attempt to have it both ways, an ambivalence within our constitutional tradition that has lasted to our own day.

Among the first important efforts to confront the alternative possibilities were the few (but since much-scrutinized) early state cases of judicial review. Two of these cases—*Trevett v. Weeden* from Rhode Island, and *Bayard v. Singleton* from North Carolina—stand out; both were controversial and widely reported just before and during the 1787 convention and hence give some evidence of the emerging attitudes about the nature and legitimacy of judicial review. In both cases, judges struck down state statutes; in both, the legislatures challenged their authority to do this; in both, the court refused to bow to legislative pressure and more or less prevailed. For purposes of establishing the background of the Chase-Iredell debate, the most interesting fact is that one of these decisions rested on an unwritten constitution, the other on a written one.

Trevett involved a Rhode Island statute that imposed a statutory penalty on those who refused to accept the state's notorious paper money in tender of debt and provided that actions to collect the penalty were to be tried without a jury. The defendant argued that this violated fundamental law, and was "a mere nullity, and void." Rhode Island was one of two states that had not framed a new constitution; and the colonial charter, which served as a constitution, did not expressly guarantee jury trial. Counsel's argument (described in a widely distributed pamphlet) was framed in terms of pure Cokean unwritten constitutionalism.[39] The court ruled for the defendant, apparently on the basis of the constitutional argument, though no written opinions survive. The judges were called before the legislature, where they refused to recant or explain their decision. Four out of five of them were replaced by the legislature the next year; but the same legislature repealed the statute those same judges had declared invalid.[40]

James Iredell had a leading role in the *Bayard* case. In 1785, the North Carolina legislature passed a law requiring summary dismissal of legal challenges to confiscations of Loyalists' property. Iredell, representing a plaintiff in one of these actions, attacked the statute as a violation of the state's constitutional guarantee of jury trial. When the judges came under political attack after a preliminary ruling intimating sympathy with his constitutional argument, he defended them in a pamphlet that anticipated Hamilton's and Marshall's later arguments for judicial review.[41] In the end, a motion to censure the judges failed; and at the next term of court, which came in the summer of 1787 while the Convention was proceeding in Philadelphia, they did invalidate the statute, explicitly on the constitutional ground Iredell had urged.[42]

The ensuing correspondence between Iredell and Richard Spaight, one of the North Carolina delegates in Philadelphia, is perhaps the most illuminating exchange on judicial review that we have from the Confederation period. It shows that while Iredell had already formulated the positivist Hamilton–Marshall theory of judicial review in 1787, he still at that time supplemented it with the Cokean theory that he would repudiate in 1798 when Chase invoked it in *Calder*.

Spaight wrote to Iredell protesting against the *Bayard* decision, news of which had just reached Philadelphia; he said that, though the law was unjust and perhaps contrary to the state constitution, nothing gave the judges authority to disregard a duly passed act of the legislature. And if they did have such authority, "the State, instead of being governed by the representatives in general Assembly, would be subject to the will of three individuals, who united in their own persons the legislative and judiciary powers, which no monarch enjoys, and which would be more despotic than the Roman Decemvirate, and equally as insufferable."[43]

Iredell replied in a long letter building on his earlier pamphlet, which bears comparison with Hamilton's *Federalist* No. 78 (written later in the year) as a persuasive exposition of what has become the standard positivist American doctrine of judicial review:

> I confess it has ever been my opinion, that an act inconsistent with the Constitution was void; and that the judges, consistently with their duties, could not carry it into effect. The Constitution appears to me to be a fundamental law, limiting the powers of the Legislature, and with which every exercise of those powers must, necessarily, be compared. . . . It is not that the judges are appointed arbiters, and to determine as it were upon any application, whether the Assembly have or have not violated the Constitution; but when an act is necessarily brought in judgment before them, they must, unavoidably, determine one way or another.

He favorably contrasted judicial review founded on a positive written constitution with more ethereal kinds; here he sounded ready to take the position he was later to articulate against Chase:

> It really appears to me, the exercise of the power is unavoidable, the Constitution not being a mere imaginary thing, about which ten thousand different opinions may be formed, but a written document to which all may have recourse, and to which, therefore, the judges cannot wilfully blind themselves.

However, he had not yet reached that position; instead, he went on to acknowledge the Cokean doctrine:

> Without an express Constitution the powers of the Legislature would undoubtedly have been absolute (as the Parliament in Great Britain is held to be), and any act passed, *not inconsistent with natural justice* (for that curb is avowed by the judges even in England), would have been binding on the people.[44]

Something between 1787 and 1798 led Iredell to change his mind about judicial enforcement of natural justice, bringing him to the rejection of Cokean judicial review that he first expressed in *Calder*. But in 1787 he was not yet ready to articulate that position. Nor, as best I can tell, was anyone else.

THE FEDERAL CONSTITUTION

Iredell's letter to Spaight is one significant clue to what articulate lawyers thought about the question of a judicially enforceable unwritten constitution at the time the federal Constitution was drafted. Like most of the rather fragmentary evidence we have, it tilts toward Chase's side; Iredell himself was not yet an Iredellian in 1787. Perhaps no one was. On the other hand there was so little attention paid to these questions in the Convention, the ratification proceedings, and later during the adoption of the Bill of Rights that the original understanding on the issue of judicial enforcement of implied constitutional limitations cannot be considered more than a tentative one.

Not only were the delegates to the Philadelphia and state ratifying conventions not concerned with the question Chase and Iredell would later debate; they were not very much concerned with whether there would be judicial review at all, though a clear majority of those who mentioned the practice assumed that it would exist.[45] But compared to such issues as the representation of the states in Congress, the structure and power of the executive, and the treatment of slavery, judicial review was very much a side-issue. Thus it is not surprising that there was no direct consideration of the still more refined question of whether judges might enforce implied as well as express constitutional limitations.

The only explicit mention of the possibility of judicial enforcement of an unwritten constitution at Philadelphia came in a brief and inconclusive exchange during the debate over the ex post facto clause. Oliver Ellsworth opposed the clause, saying "there was no lawyer, no civilian who would not say that ex post facto laws were void of themselves. It can not then be necessary to prohibit them." James Wilson agreed; to prohibit such laws would "proclaim that we are ignorant of the first principles of Legislation." On the other side, Daniel Carroll of Maryland noted that whatever "civilians or others" might say, state legislatures had passed such laws and they had taken effect. Hugh Williamson of North Carolina said that the similar clause in his state's constitution, "tho it has been violated . . . has done good there and may do good here, because the Judges can take hold of it."[46]

What can we infer from these fragmentary remarks? Ellsworth certainly presupposed traditional Cokean implied limitation doctrines, fortified by contemporary European civil law theory. While he did not say explicitly that judges would disregard a "void" law, his use of that legal term suggested judicial review, and he later endorsed judicial review in the Connecticut ratification debate.[47]

Wilson, an especially well-educated and cosmopolitan lawyer, was worried that express prohibition of what the best theorists considered a legal absurdity would expose Americans to ridicule; neither this nor Carroll's counter that high-toned theory had not always controlled legislative practice had any clear implication one way or the other for judicial review. Only Williamson explicitly referred to judicial enforcement, and the implication of his remark for the unwritten constitution is not clear. He might have meant that in practice judges' spines would be stiffened to do what would be their duty in any case if they had written constitutional language to "take hold of"; or he might have thought what Iredell would later say, that judges could only exercise judicial review on the basis of express constitutional provisions.

The most extensive discussion of judicial review at the Convention came in connection with the proposal to vest what later became the presidential veto in a council of revision made up of the president and the justices of the Supreme Court. Madison, Wilson, and George Mason, among others, favored this proposal. Opponents said that the justices would exercise their check on Congress through judicial review, and there was no need to give them a "double negative." To this, Wilson, backed by Mason, responded: "Laws may be unjust, may be unwise, may be dangerous, may be destructive; and yet not be so unconstitutional as to justify the Judges in refusing to give them effect."[48]

Wilson's reference to laws that were unjust but not subject to judicial invalidation might suggest an Iredellian position, but other evidence makes this unlikely. Only three years later, in a celebrated series of public lectures, he was to endorse the *Bonham's Case* doctrine that judges should invalidate legislation inconsistent with common right and reason, adding that Americans had placed "another control" on legislative authority—judicial enforcement of a written Constitution.[49] This was a clear endorsement of the Chase position. More likely, Wilson meant by his Convention statement that laws sufficiently unjust for justices to veto when acting as revisers would nevertheless not be "*so* unconstitutional as to justify" judicial invalidation. It was a commonplace during this period of the emergence of judicial review—both Chase and Iredell said it—that it was an "awful power," which should only be exercised "in a very clear case."[50]

That is about as much as can be found in the Convention

debates on the issue of the Chase–Iredell debate. In the ratification debates that followed, a number of spokesmen on both sides
assumed there would be judicial review; but again, not surprisingly, no one answered one way or the other on the question of
whether adoption of a written constitution was consistent with
judicial enforcement of unwritten fundamental law. The nearest
approach came in the exchanges over the failure of the Constitution to contain a bill of rights; these are worth some attention,
particularly as they provide the most immediate background for
the later enactment of the Ninth Amendment.

THE BILL OF RIGHTS AND THE NINTH AMENDMENT

Many of the state constitutions had contained separate and
extensive bills of rights. But the Federalists of 1787 were not
enthusiastic to extend this practice to the national constitution.
The reasons for the reluctance are not entirely clear. Some of the
delegates were all-out nationalists, and they may have wished to
leave the powers of the new general government as nearly unre-
stricted as possible. Many of them were devout political realists,
skeptical of the effectiveness of high-sounding declarations to
restrain power; they believed much more in the machinery of
representation, separation of powers, and checks and balances as
safeguards against tyranny than in what Hamilton called "apho-
risms . . . which would sound much better in a treatise of ethics
than in a constitution of government."[51]

Whatever the reasons, when toward the end of the Convention
George Mason moved that a bill of rights be added to the Constitution, not one delegation supported him.[52] On the other hand, a
number of provisions protecting individual rights had been included in the body of the document. In addition to the ex post
facto clause, already mentioned, there were the habeas corpus and
bill of attainder clauses of Article I, Section 9; ex post facto, bill
of attainder, and contract clauses restraining the states in Article
I, Section 10; and in Article III a guarantee of trial by jury in
criminal cases, and a restrictive definition of treason.

The omission of a full bill of rights gave the Antifederalists one
of their most effective arguing points in opposing ratification.
Even Jefferson disapproved; he wrote Madison from Paris, "A bill
of rights is what the people are entitled to against any govern-

ment on earth, general or particular, and what no just government should refuse, or rest on inference."[53]

Hamilton gave a standard Federalist response on the question of a bill of rights. His argument, derived from an earlier formulation of James Wilson's, stands in the great tradition of the lawyer who pleads alibi, self-defense, and insanity all at once.[54] After arguing that the few existing guarantees constituted a satisfactory bill of rights, he could not resist adding that a bill of rights was unnecessary and indeed would even be dangerous—unnecessary, because the federal government was confined to its granted powers, and had no power to violate rights; dangerous, because to state explicit prohibitions could suggest by negative implication that what was not prohibited was thereby granted.

This opened up two lines of Antifederalist response. First, if explicit restrictions were unnecessary, even dangerous, why were trial by jury, habeas corpus, and the like guaranteed? To this the Federalists never developed a convincing response. Second, limiting Congress to its granted powers hardly seemed sufficient to protect basic rights—particularly given the necessary-and-proper clause, and the failure to repeat the Articles of Confederation's restriction of national legislative powers to those "expressly" granted. After all, many measures violating traditional rights might be useful in implementing the granted powers, if a broad concept of implied powers were adopted. Congress had the express power to punish counterfeiting; why under this power could it not provide for general warrants to detect counterfeiters, secret trials without counsel to convict them, and drawing and quartering to punish them?

The Federalists *did* have an answer to this line of argument; they invoked the traditional Cokean doctrine of implied limitations on legislative power. Consistent with the arguments that they and their fellow Americans had pressed against Parliament as colonists, they argued that the grants of power to Congress were implicitly limited by individual rights. Thus Theophilus Parsons argued that "no power was given to Congress to infringe on any one of the natural rights of the people by this Constitution; and should they attempt it without constitutional authority, the act would be a nullity, and could not be enforced."[55] One might restate this as a construction of the necessary and proper clause; laws passed by Congress must be both instrumentally useful in pursuing one of Congress's delegated powers (necessary) and consistent with traditionally recognized principles of individual right (proper). While the sovereign people could grant their government any powers they wished, including the power to violate natural rights (as they did, for instance, in authorizing slavery), no such power should rest on implication; a power to violate basic rights must be stated in explicit terms.

Madison's *Federalist* No. 44 further illustrates the standard Federalist assumption of implied limitations, in this case as applied to the legislative powers of the states. Discussing the ex post facto, bill of attainder, and contract clauses of Article I, Section 10, he said that the state laws they prohibited were "contrary to the first principles of the social compact." While only some laws of these kinds were expressly prohibited by state constitutions, "all of them are prohibited by the spirit and scope of these fundamental charters." In fact, no state constitution contained a contract clause; Madison's point was that by virtue of their republican "spirit and scope," and independent of their express provisions, all of them implied its unwritten equivalent. The written federal prohibitions of Article I, Section 10, then provided "*additional* fences against these dangers."[56]

Against this standard Cokean doctrine, some of the Antifederalists pressed the newer Blackstonian position that legislative authority was presumptively unlimited, so that legislative power—whether general as with the states or confined to enumerated areas as with the federal government—encompassed everything within the scope of the grant that was not explicitly withheld. Rights, in this view, were only retained if stated; to omit stating them was to risk surrendering them into the hands of the legislature. The Federalists stressed the contrary risk that an explicit enumeration of rights risked being read as a repudiation of traditional Cokean notions, thus excluding the rights not enumerated.

In the event, the Federalists won the struggle and the Constitution was ratified, though only narrowly and, in the key states of New York and Virginia, only after its proponents promised a future bill of rights. It was Madison who undertook to deliver on this promise during the First Congress, and in his drafting of what were to become the first ten amendments to the Constitution he took account of the warnings Federalists had given about the negative implications that might be drawn from an enumeration of rights. The memory of these arguments led him to include among his proposals what eventually became the Ninth Amendment, as is shown by his explanation of his measure to the House:

> It has been objected also against a bill of rights, that, by enumerating particular exceptions to the grant of power, it would disparage those rights which were not placed in that enumeration; and it might follow, by implication, that those rights which were not singled out, were intended to be assigned into the hands of the General Government, and were consequently insecure. This is one of the most plausible arguments I have ever heard urged against the admission of a bill of rights into this system; but, I conceive, that it may be guarded against [by the proposed amendment].[57]

Now recall the words of the amendment as finally enacted: "The enumeration in this Constitution, of certain rights, shall not be construed to deny or disparage others retained by the people." This is a canon of construction, and its purpose is clear given the background of the earlier Federalist defenses of the omission of a bill of rights. It provides that the grants of federal power are to be construed according to the Cokean rather than the Blackstonian notion of legislative sovereignty, thus rejecting the presumption that legislative powers are unlimited unless expressly qualified. Constitutional rights—conceived as areas of potential regulation exempted from the reach of legislative powers that otherwise might be read to include them—are not confined to those enumerated in the document. The grants of power are to be interpreted as subject to the implicit limitations placed by whatever rights properly qualify them, whether or not those rights have themselves been reduced to enacted form. These unenumerated rights form an unwritten constitution.

An example may help to clarify the point analytically. Suppose Congress adopted for the District of Columbia a debtor stay law that would have violated the contract clause if adopted by a state. Under the canon of construction laid down by the Ninth Amendment, the absence of a similar explicit prohibition restraining Congress would not mean that such laws automatically passed muster; creditors could still argue that the plenary legislative powers granted by the seat-of-government clause should be interpreted as limited by the traditional but (as against the federal government) unenumerated right to be free of unwarranted infringements of contractual claims—the right that Madison believed had put this kind of debtor relief legislation beyond the "spirit and scope" even of state constitutions, though none of those constitutions expressly prohibited it.[58]

The Ninth Amendment worked to supplement the Tenth in comforting those fearful of the new national government. The Tenth Amendment explicitly confirmed that the federal government was confined to its enumerated powers. On the other hand, it carried forward the Convention's rejection of the Antifederalist insistence that, as had been the case under the Articles of Confederation, Congress should be confined to powers "expressly delegated." Central to the Federalist position was the idea that implied powers must be admitted if the central government were to function effectively. The existence of implied federal powers, however, excited fears that they would render rights insecure. It was these fears that the Ninth Amendment addressed by providing that powers, including implied powers, should be construed subject to the implied limitations provided by the natural and traditional rights that Americans were so used to invoking.

On this interpretation, the Ninth Amendment did not by itself operate as a federal constitutional limitation on state power. For example, it would not have occurred to Chase to cite it in his debate with Iredell. Madison and his contemporaries doubtless would have thought of it only in connection with issues of implied limitation on the grants of federal power. At the same time, both Chase and Madison, as *Calder* and *Federalist* No. 44 show, thought the powers of state legislatures were subject to the same implied limitations that the Ninth Amendment affirmed as restraints on federal power. But these limitations on the states preexisted the adoption of the federal Constitution, and gained no additional legal force from its adoption.[59]

This is not to say, though, that if we project the Ninth Amendment's language and purposes into a future not foreseen in 1791, it cannot properly lend support to a broad construction of the "privileges or immunities," and rights of "life, liberty, or property" guaranteed against state power by the Fourteenth Amendment. Given the transformed scope of federal protection of individuals against the states that followed from the Civil War, the general canon of construction supplied by the Ninth Amendment under-writes interpreting Section One of the Fourteenth Amendment as finally incorporating into the federal Constitution the implied limitations on state legislative power that from the beginning had been regarded as a matter of general state constitutional law.[60]

But the most direct application of the Ninth Amendment is to affirm that the delegated federal powers should be construed in Cokean terms, as subject to implied limitation by basic though unenumerated rights. Today, it is standard to identify those implied limitations as the substantive rights of liberty and property protected under the modern broad construction of the due process clause of the Fifth Amendment, which is held to impose on the federal government the same limitations imposed on the states under Section One of the Fourteenth Amendment.[61] The Ninth Amendment as originally understood supports that construction of the due process clause, which is treated not as the source but as the textual shelter for fundamental implied rights.[62]

This returns us to our beginning point, the Chase–Iredell exchange of 1798. What startles modern lawyers about this exchange is the frankness of Chase's appeal to an unwritten constitution. But it takes only a little familiarity with the customary discourse of his time to remove any sense of surprise at this appeal; he was articulating a traditional orthodoxy. What seems genuinely more surprising, in light of the changes that had taken place in the American conception of constitutional government after 1776, is how few of his contemporaries supported Iredell.

Yet I have found no other explicit statements of the Iredell view during the federal and early national periods. During this time, some (though an ever-decreasing number) agreed with Spaight in total opposition to judicial review across the board. A much more impressive array of voices confirmed Chase's doctrine that judges were to enforce implied limitations based on natural law and common law tradition as well as the written constitution—among them such major commentators as James Wilson, St. George Tucker, and James Kent.[63] Kent and other leading state judges invoked Cokean judicial review in state constitutional cases to protect property and vested rights beyond what written constitutions provided.[64] Story and his contemporaries on the federal bench likewise followed Chase in affirming that general unwritten principles took precedence over state legislation.[65]

And finally John Marshall himself in *Fletcher v. Peck* led a unanimous Supreme Court in striking down the Georgia legislature's attempt to undo the corrupt sale of the state's western lands, stating as one of the two alternative grounds for the decision "general principles that are common to our free institutions." The other ground foreshadowed one way in which the courts would eventually domesticate implied constitutional limitations within the shelter of the text; Marshall strained to bring what he saw as a violation of vested rights under the contract clause, just as later judges would make law-of-the-land and due process clauses the textual vehicles of choice for implied rights. Marshall's Jeffersonian colleague William Johnson, apparently feeling no uneasiness about judicial review on the basis of a purely unwritten supplemental constitution, protested the strained textual construction while concurring in the result on the basis of unwritten general principles alone.[66]

One might conclude from all this that Chase's position *was* the Founders' understanding on the question of the unwritten constitution. In a sense it was. But here, as so often, we lawyers are likely to leap too confidently to historical conclusions. In its early stages, the working theory of judicial review was still unformed and volatile.[67] However unusual Iredell's ability to articulate an exclusively positivist theory of judicial review may have been in 1798, his approach was latent in a newly emerging constitutional consensus that combined belief in popular sovereignty with distrust of discretion in the hands of a conservative and nationalizing judiciary. Iredell was no isolated eccentric, but an accomplished lawyer and solid citizen of his time, perhaps a little in advance of his contemporaries in pressing the claims of legal positivism in constitutional law. Today, when constitutional positivism is the background orthodoxy from which other approaches to judicial review must justify deviation, it is particularly important to see how different things were at the beginning, when the notion of implied limitations was the conventional wisdom. But on the question Iredell and Chase debated, perhaps the deepest original understanding was that the question was debatable.

Notes

1. For more on what I mean by this question, and for some earlier attempts to address it, see my "Do We Have an Unwritten Constitution?" *Stanford Law Review* 27 (1975): 703–18; "Origins of the Unwritten Constitution: Fundamental Law in American Revolutionary Thought," *Stanford Law Review* 30 (1978): 843–93; and "The Constitution as Scripture," *Stanford Law Review* 37 (1984): 1–25.

2. Thurgood Marshall, "The Constitution's Bicentennial: Commemorating the Wrong Document?" *Vanderbilt Law Review* 40 (1987): 1337, 1340.

3. I wrote this essay without the benefit of having read Suzanna Sherry's fine article "The Founders' Unwritten Constitution," *University of Chicago Law Review* 54 (1987): 1127–77. Professor Sherry goes over much of the same ground I do and independently reaches largely similar conclusions. As I read her, we differ on some points of interpretive detail; and, more than I, she believes that the Founders can still speak across the centuries to us today.

4. This is the interpretation offered in Russell Caplan, "The History and Meaning of the Ninth Amendment," *Virginia Law Review* 69 (1983): 223–68. During his confirmation hearings, Judge Bork suggested that he found this the most plausible interpretation of the amendment.

5. 3 Dall. (3 U.S.) 386 (1796). For purposes of this essay, I bypass the question of whether the events of the 1790s affected the understanding of this issue reflected in the Chase–Iredell exchange. The extra power conferred on a (largely Federalist) judiciary by broad conceptions of "unwritten law" did increasingly become matters of public partisan struggle during those years with the emergence of issues such as the Yazoo lands scandal and the controversy over whether the Constitution authorized a federal common law of crimes.

6. For an account of the practice of "equitable" legislative oversight in Connecticut, see the various opinions in Calder v. Bull itself; for recognition of a similar practice in Rhode Island, see Olney v. Arnold, 3 Dall. (3 U.S.) 308 (1796). On the legislative exercise of judicial functions during the colonial period and afterward, see generally Gordon Wood, *The Creation of the American Republic, 1776–1787* (Chapel Hill: University of North Carolina Press, 1969), 154–55, and sources there cited.

7. 3 Dall. (3 U.S.) 386 (1796), 390–94. While agreeing that the ex post facto clause extended only to criminal laws, Justice Paterson added his view, contrary to Chase's, that "retrospective laws of every description . . . neither accord with sound legislation, nor the fundamental principles of the social compact." Ibid., 397. He thought the Connecticut legislature's action in this case did not violate this principle, since it was exercising a genuinely judicial function allocated to it in the state's customary constitution. Ibid., 395–96. Justice Iredell agreed with Chase that civil retrospective legislation was sometimes necessary and just (ibid., 400) and likewise agreed with his construction of the ex post facto clause.

8. Ibid., 388.

9. Chase made the second point explicitly (ibid., 394); I read him to make the first when he writes: "Whether the legislature of any of the states can revise and correct by law, a decision of any of its courts of justice, although not prohibited by the constitution of the state, is a question of very great importance, and not necessary now to be determined; because the resolution or law in question does not go so far." Ibid., 387.

10. Ibid., 387–88 (emphasis added).

11. Ibid., 387.

12. The "empire of laws" phrase comes from James Harrington, "The Commonwealth of Oceana," in J. G. A. Pocock, ed., *The Political Works of James Harrington* (Cambridge, Eng.: Cambridge University Press, 1977). It was reshaped into its familiar modern form by John Adams. See Massachusetts Constitution, Declaration of Rights, Article 30 (1780), which requires the separation of executive, legislative, and judicial powers "to the end that it shall be a government of laws, and not of men." The debate over the relative merits of government "of law" and "of men" is not modern, of course, nor associated with "liberalism," but forms a central theme in Plato's *Republic, Statesman,* and *Laws,* and in Aristotle's *Politics.*

It seems that the doctrine of separation of powers has often operated in American constitutional discourse to mediate between classical republican (Aristotelian, Harringtonian) doctrines of balanced government and government under law, and liberal (Lockean) doctrines of individual natural rights. Americans never experienced the wall of separation presupposed by J. G. A. Pocock when he writes that "the basic concept in republican thinking is *virtus;* the basic concept of all jurisprudence is necessarily *jus;* and there is no known way of representing virtue as a right." Pocock, "Cambridge Paradigms and Scotch Philosophers: A Study of the Relations between the Civic Humanist and the Civil Jurisprudential Interpretation of Eighteenth-Century Social Thought," in Istvan Hont and Michael Ignatieff, eds., *Wealth and Virtue: The Shaping of Political Economy in the Scottish Enlightenment* (Cambridge, Eng.: Cambridge University Press, 1983), 248.

13. Fletcher v. Peck, 6 Cranch (10 U.S.) 87, 136 (1810); Dartmouth College v. Woodward, 4 Wheat. (17 U.S.) 518, 581 (1819); Taylor v. Porter, 4 Hill 140, 147 (1840); Thomas Cooley, *A Treatise on the Constitutional Limitations Which Rest upon the Legislative Power of the States of the American Union* (Boston: Little, Brown & Co., 1868), 357. See generally Edward Corwin, "The Basic Doctrine of American Constitutional Law," *Michigan Law Review* 12 (1914): 247–76.

14. It is a mistake that we owe to Progressive and New Deal lawyers and historians to think that (what we would call) substantive due process was mainly an innovation of the "*Lochner* era." See Edward Corwin, "The Doctrine of Due Process of Law before the Civil War," *Harvard Law Review* 24 (1911): 366–85, 460–79; Walton Hamilton, "The Path of Due Process of Law," in Conyers Read, ed., *The Constitution Reconsidered* (New York: Columbia University Press, 1938), 167–90. The idea that legislative infringement of property rights "substantively" (as we would say) violates state law-of-the-land or due process clauses appeared very early and gained steadily increasing acceptance throughout the nineteenth century. See, for early appearances, Lindsay v. Commissioners, 2 Bay (S.C.) 38 (1796); University of North Carolina v. Foy, 5 N.C. 53 (1805); Little v. Frost, 3 Mass. R. 106 (1807). By the period of Reconstruction, courts in at least twenty-one states had applied or approved the application of due process or law-of-the-land clauses in a "substantive" sense, typically to prohibit infringement of vested rights. See *In re* Dorsey, 34 Ala. 311 (1838); *Ex Parte* Martin, 13 Ark. 198 (1853); Sherman v. Buck, 32 Cal. 432 (1867); McNealy v. Gregory, 13 Fla. 417 (1871); Loughborough v. Harris, 42 Ga. 500 (1871); Lane v. Dorman, 3 Scam. (Ill.) 238 (1841); Beebe v. State, 6 Ind. 501 (1855); Reed v. Wright, 2

Greene (Ia.) 15 (1849); Gaines v. Buford, 1 Dana (31 Ky.) 481 (1833); Allen v. Jay, 60 Me. 124 (1872); Regents v. Williams, 9 G. & J. (Md.) 233 (1838); Denny v. Mattoon, 84 Mass. 361 (1861); Ames v. Port Huron Co., 11 Mich. 139 (1863); Baker v. Kelley, 11 Minn. 358 (1866); Wright v. Cradlebaugh, 3 Nev. 341 (1867); Opinion of the Judges, 4 N.H. 565 (1827); Matter of John and Cherry Streets, 19 Wend. (N.Y.) 679 (1839); Hoke v. Henderson, 15 N.C. 1 (1833); Brown v. Hummel, 6 Pa. St. 86 (1847); Dunn v. Charleston, Harper (S.C.) 189 (1824); Wally's Heirs v. Kennedy, 10 Tenn. 554 (1831).

15. Calder v. Bull, 3 Dall. 386, 398–99 (1798). Iredell gave a more extended statement of his view in a case decided on circuit in June of the same year, after argument in Calder, but before the decision was announced. He reiterated that "the words 'against natural justice' are very loose terms" and added that if the framers of the constitution (of North Carolina, which was the one involved in the case) had "intended . . . to leave it to the courts, in all instances, to say whether an act was agreeable to natural justice or not, this restriction would have been inserted, together with others." Minge v. Gilmour, 17 Fed. Cas. 440, 443–44 (C.C.D.N.C., 1798).

16. For an expanded and fully documented statement of the argument of this section, see Grey, "Origins of the Unwritten Constitution."

17. Quoted by Julius Goebel, *History of the United States Supreme Court: Antecedents and Beginnings to 1801* (New York: Macmillan, 1971), 89.

18. Letter from John Adams to Thomas Jefferson, August 24, 1815, in Charles Francis Adams, ed., *The Works of John Adams*, 10 vols. (Boston: Little, Brown & Co., 1850–56), 10:172–73.

19. Letter of John Adams to William Tudor (March 29, 1817), in ibid., 247–48; for Otis's argument see Adams's notes, ibid., 2:521. The usage reflected in Otis's argument, which equated the constitution with fundamental law, coexisted during this period with the alternative English usage according to which the constitution was made up of extralegal conventions. Thus, in keeping with the latter usage John Adams wrote that "legally" the king could prevent Parliament from sitting and the Commons could paralyze the monarchy by withholding supply, but these actions would be "unconstitutional." Letter from John Adams to *Boston Gazette*, February 8, 1773, in ibid., 3:556.

20. 77 Eng. Rep. 647 (C.P., 1610).

21. 77 Eng. Rep. 377, 392 (K.B. 1609); and see Day v. Savadge, 80 Eng. Rep. 235 (K.B. 1614).

22. 3 Howell's State Trials 825, 1235 (1637).

23. See Adams, *Works of John Adams*, 2:522.

24. William Blackstone, *Commentaries on the Laws of England*, 4 vols. (Oxford, Eng.: Clarendon Press, 1765–69), 1:41.

25. Ibid., 49, 147, 160-61.

26. Ibid., 91.

27. Speech of Alderman Beckford, quoted in John Gough, *Fundamental Law in English History* (Oxford, Eng.: Clarendon Press, 1955), 194; speech of Lord Camden, February 10, 1766, in *Parliamentary History of England*, 36 vols. (London, 1813), 16:178. See also the speech of Lord Chatham, January 20, 1775, in ibid., 18:165.

28. Letter of Thomas Jefferson to James Madison, February 17, 1826, in Paul L. Ford, ed., *The Writings of Thomas Jefferson*, 10 vols. (New York: G. P. Putnam & Sons, 1892–99), 10:376.

29. Edward Coke, *Institutes of the Laws of England*, 3 vols. (Philadelphia: Johnson and Walnen, 1812), 3:111.

30. John Rushworth, *Historical Collections,* 8 vols. (London: T. Newcomb, 1659–1701), 1:562.

31. Jean Jacques Burlamaqui, *The Principles of Natural and Politic Law,* 5th ed., trans. T. Nugent (Cambridge, Mass.: Harvard University Press, 1807), 45–47.

32. Emmerich de Vattel, *The Law of Nations,* trans. Charles G. Fenwick (Washington, D.C.: Carnegie Institution, 1916), 19.

33. Cited from Wood, *Creation of the American Republic,* 266–67.

34. See the treatment of these developments, ibid., 306–89.

35. The most complete treatment of the disputes over judicial review during the Confederation period is in William W. Crosskey and William Jeffrey, Jr., *Politics and the Constitution in the History of the United States,* 3 vols. (Chicago: University of Chicago Press, 1953–80), 2:944–75.

36. Francis Thorpe, *The Federal and State Constitutions, Colonial Charters, and Other Organic Laws,* 7 vols. (Washington, D.C.: Government Printing Office, 1909), 3:1889 (emphasis added). The parallel provision of the Pennsylvania constitution was cited as a ground for invalidating legislation that "took from A to give to B" by Justice Paterson in Van Horne's Lessee v. Dorrance, 2 Dall. (2 U.S.) 304, 310 (1795), and nineteenth-century courts sporadically cited similar "inalienable rights" clauses in support of decisions protecting property rights against legislative intrusion. See, for example, Billings v. Hall, 7 Cal. 1 (1857); Beebe v. State, 6 Ind. 501 (1855); Hanson v. Vernon, 27 Ia. 28 (1869); Proprietors of Kennebec v. Laboree, 2 Greenl. (Me.) 275 (1823); Lessee of Good v. Zercher, 12 Oh. 364 (1843); Crenshaw v. State River Co., 27 Va. 245 (1828); Durkee v. City of Janesville, 28 Wis. 464 (1871).

37. Max Farrand, ed., *Records of the Federal Convention of 1787,* rev. ed., 4 vols. (New Haven, Conn.: Yale University Press, 1966), 1:133–34 [hereafter referred to as Farrand, *Records*].

38. See Thomas Jefferson, *Notes on the State of Virginia* (New York: W. W. Norton, 1972), 120: "173 despots would surely be as oppressive as one. . . . An *elective despotism* was not the government we fought for . . .".

39. See Peleg Chandler, *American Criminal Trials,* 2 vols. (Boston: Little, Brown & Co., 1844), 2:283, 304–19.

40. See the account in Crosskey and Jeffrey, *Politics and the Constitution,* 2:965–68.

41. Griffith McRee, *The Life and Correspondence of James Iredell,* 2 vols. (New York: D. Appleton, 1857–58), 2:145–49.

42. Bayard v. Singleton, 1 Martin (N.C.) 42 (1787). See the account in Crosskey and Jeffrey, *Politics and the Constitution,* 2:971–74.

43. McRee, *Life and Correspondence of Iredell,* 2:169.

44. Ibid., 172–74 (emphasis added).

45. See the count of delegates in Raoul Berger, *Congress vs. the Supreme Court* (Cambridge: Harvard University Press, 1969), 47–48.

46. Farrand, *Records,* 2:375–76.

47. Merrill Jensen, ed., *Documentary History of the Ratification of the Constitution,* 15 vols. (Madison: State Historical Society of Wisconsin, 1976–), 13:553.

48. Farrand, *Records,* 2:73.

49. Robert McCloskey, ed., *The Works of James Wilson,* 2 vols. (Cambridge, Mass.: Harvard University Press, 1967), 1:326–29.

50. Iredell in Calder v. Bull, 3 Dall. (3 U.S.) 386, 399 (1798) (judicial review is a "delicate and awful" power, which the court should only resort to "in a clear and urgent

case"); Chase in Hylton v. United States, 3 Dall. (3 U.S.) 171, 175 (1796) (judicial review only appropriate "in a very clear case").

51. *Federalist* 84:513.

52. Farrand, *Records,* 2:587–88.

53. Letter of Thomas Jefferson to James Madison December 20, 1787, in Julian Boyd, ed., *The Papers of Thomas Jefferson,* 20 vols. (Princeton, N.J.: Princeton University Press, 1950–), 12:440.

54. *Federalist* 84 (Hamilton); Jensen, *Documentary History of Ratification,* 2:168 (Wilson).

55. Jonathan Elliot, ed., *The Debates in the Several State Conventions on the Adoption of the Federal Constitution,* 2d ed., 5 vols. (Philadelphia: J. B. Lippincott, 1901), 3:443.

56. *Federalist* 44:282 (emphasis added).

57. *Annals of Congress,* 1:451–52.

58. The Supreme Court has since held that restraints similar to those imposed upon the states by the contract clause bind Congress under the due process clause; see Louisville Joint Stock Land Bank v. Radford, 295 U.S. 555 (1935), but compare Pension Benefit Guaranty Co. v. R. A. Gray and Co., 467 U.S. 717 (1984).

59. Later it became common to make the assumption of implied limitations on state legislative power explicit by inserting the language of the Ninth Amendment into new state constitutions as they were adopted; John Ely lists twenty-six such "little Ninth Amendments" in *Democracy and Distrust* (Cambridge, Mass.: Harvard University Press, 1980), 203.

60. In support of this, it might be noted that a number of state courts had referred to their state "little Ninth Amendments" as additional support in substantive due process cases decided before or immediately after the ratification of the Fourteenth Amendment. See, e.g., *In re* Dorsey, 7 Port (Ala.) 293 (1838); *Ex Parte* Martin, 13 Ark. 198 (1853); Sherman v. Buck, 32 Cal. 241 (1867); Hanson v. Vernon, 27 Iowa 28 (1869).

61. As in Bolling v. Sharpe, 347 U.S. 497 (1954); and see Buckley v. Valeo, 424 U.S. 1, 93 (1976) ("Equal protection analysis in the Fifth Amendment area is the same as under the Fourteenth Amendment").

62. Of course, original meaning need not control today; contemporary opponents of an unwritten constitution might argue, though few of them do, that because contemporary lawyers' conception of law is more positivistic than the Founders' conception, we should update our living constitution by no longer countenancing the judicial enforcement of unenumerated rights.

63. Wilson, "Lectures on Law," in McCloskey, ed., *Works,* 1:326–29 [full citation at note 49]; Henry St. George Tucker, ed., *Blackstone's Commentaries on the Laws of England,* 2 vols. (Philadelphia: William Young Birch & Abraham Small, 1803), 1:153A; James Kent, *Commentaries on American Law,* 4 vols. (New York: O. Halsted, 1826–30), 1:448, 455.

64. Gardner v. Newburgh, 2 Johns. Ch. (N.Y.) 162 (1816); Holden v. James, 11 Mass. 396 (1814); Bowman v. Middleton, 1 Bay (S.C.) 252 (1793); Merrill v. Sherburne, 1 N.H. 199 (1819). See generally Corwin, "Basic Doctrine"; J. A. C. Grant, "The Higher Law Background of the Law of Eminent Domain," *Wisconsin Law Review* 6 (1931): 69.

65. Terrett v. Taylor, 9 Cranch (13 U.S.) 43 (1815); Wilkinson v. Leland, 2 Pet. (27 U.S.) 627 (1829); and see Van Horne's Lessee v. Dorrance, 2 Dall. (2 U.S.) 304 (1795).

66. Fletcher v. Peck, 6 Cranch (10 U.S.) 87 (1810).

67. Sylvia Snowiss gives the best account (that I know) of that volatility in her fine unpublished paper, "From Fundamental Law to the Supreme Law of the Land: A Reinterpretation of the Origin of Judicial Review in the United States" (1981) (on file with author).

Further Reading

There is a seemingly endless shelf of literature on the drafting and adoption of the Constitution. The annotated list that follows includes some of the more important sources and later studies. Most of these can be found in good college and *unusually* good public libraries. A fair number are in print as paperbacks; a few can be found in well-stocked bookstores.

Max Farrand, ed., *The Records of the Federal Convention of 1787,* rev. ed., 4 vols. (New Haven: Yale University Press, 1966), with the *Supplement* edited by James Hutson (New Haven: Yale University Press, 1987), includes the official proceedings of the Philadelphia Convention as well as the surviving private notes and journal entries made by the delegates there. James Madison's own *Notes of Debates in the Federal Convention of 1787,* first published in 1840, is currently in print in several paperback editions, notably that by the Ohio University Press, published in 1966 with an introduction by Adrienne Koch, reissued by W. W. Norton in 1987. Philip Kurland and Ralph Lerner, eds., *The Founders' Constitution,* 5 vols. (Chicago: University of Chicago Press, 1987), draws from many sources to illustrate the Founders' views on key issues; Michael Kammen, ed., *The Origins of the American Constitution: A Documentary History* (New York: Penguin Books, 1986) is a good one-volume sampler of Federalist and Antifederalist writings.

There are at least a dozen dependable secondary accounts of the Convention, including, notably, Clinton Rossiter, *1787: The Grand Convention* (New York: Macmillan, 1966) and Carl Van Doren, *The Great Rehearsal* (New York: Viking Press, 1948). Catherine Drinker Bowen's *Miracle at Philadelphia* (Boston: Little, Brown & Co., 1966) is widely considered the best narrative account; William Peters's recent *A More Perfect Union* (New York: Crown, 1987) has sold well; Richard B. Bernstein and Kym S. Rice, *Are We To Be A Nation?* (Cambridge, Mass.: Harvard University Press, 1987) nicely combines a brief text with dozens of illustrations. Forrest McDonald, *Novus Ordo Seclorum* (Lawrence: University Press of Kansas, 1985) also discusses the Convention, but McDonald was even more concerned with identifying the sources of American constitutional thought.

The Federalist, Alexander Hamilton, James Madison, and John Jay's attempt to defend and explain the Constitution, has often been reprinted—complete, and excerpts from it. Jacob Cooke, ed., *The Federalist* (Middletown, Conn.: Wesleyan University Press, 1961) is perhaps the most respected hardbound edition; there are several paperbound reissues in print, including the annotated selection in Roy Fairfield, ed., *The Federalist Papers* (Baltimore: Johns Hopkins University Press, 1981); and *The Federalist Papers: Alexander Hamilton, James Madison, John Jay,* with an introduction, annotated table of contents, and index of ideas by Clinton Rossiter (New York: New American Library, 1961), which edition is cited by page in this and other volumes of the BYU lecture series. Morton White, *Philosophy,* The Federalist, *and the Constitution* (New York: Oxford University Press, 1987); David Epstein, *The Political Theory of* The Federalist (Chicago: University of Chicago Press, 1984); and Garry Wills, *Explaining America* (New York: Doubleday, 1981) have all plumbed the depths of "Publius's" arguments. Albert Furtwangler, *The Authority of Publius* (Ithaca, N.Y.: Cornell University Press, 1984) urges caution in using the *Federalist* as the clearest expression of the Founders' thought. Furtwangler's caution about the *Federalist* should be kept in mind when looking at all of the documents associated with the Founding. We cannot be certain if official notes ever recorded comments verbatim; similarly, the journals kept by participants in the Philadelphia Convention were in some cases altered—by the authors themselves or later editors—before they were published. The proceedings of the state ratifying conventions must also be used cautiously.

Antifederalist writings have been gathered and edited by Herbert Storing in *The Complete Anti-Federalist,* 7 vols. (Chicago: University of Chicago Press, 1981), which is not really "complete" although extensive. Storing explains what critics of the

Constitution had in common with its defenders as well as what set them apart in the first volume in the collection, reprinted separately as *What the Anti-Federalists Were For* (Chicago: University of Chicago Press, 1981). Murray Dry, who was an editorial assistant for Storing's earlier compilation, has since taken portions from the larger collection for *The Anti-Federalist* (Chicago: University of Chicago Press, 1985). Also see the essay and collection in Cecelia Kenyon, ed., *The Antifederalists* (Indianapolis: Bobbs-Merrill Co., 1966). Walter Hartwell Bennett edited *Letters from the Federal Farmer to the Republican* (University: University of Alabama Press, 1978), a series often called the best Antifederalist critique of the Constitution. John Manley et al., eds., *The Case against the Constitution* (Armonk, N.Y.: M. E. Sharpe, 1987) includes critiques made in the Antifederalist tradition from 1787 to our own day. Ferdinand Lundberg, *Cracks in the Constitution* (Secaucus, N.J.: Lyle Stuart, 1980) is one example of a modern critique, with Lundberg fearing that the United States is becoming a "banana republic." Paul Finkelman, *An Imperfect Union* (Chapel Hill: University of North Carolina Press, 1981) examines the problems that arose because of the Constitution's implicit endorsement of slavery.

Americans in 1787 divided on the issue of whether the Constitution fulfilled or frustrated the principles of 1776; so have later historians. Benjamin Fletcher Wright's position is clear in the title of his *Consensus and Continuity, 1776–1787* (Boston: Boston University Press, 1958). Merrill Jensen, *The Articles of Confederation* (Madison: University of Wisconsin Press, 1940) argues for the workability of the Articles, which Jensen believes were a better expression of Revolutionary American ideals. Jensen has sometimes been called a "neo-Beardian" because he followed the lead of Charles A. Beard, *An Economic Interpretation of the Constitution of the United States* (New York: Macmillan, 1913). "Perhaps no other book on the Constitution has been more severely criticized, and so little read," Beard complained in his preface to the 1935 edition. Jackson Turner Main, *The Antifederalists* (Chapel Hill: University of North Carolina Press, 1961) tries to breathe new life into Beard's controversial argument, which Robert E. Brown scrutinizes in detail in *Charles Beard and the Constitution* (Princeton, N.J.: Princeton University Press, 1956). Forrest McDonald, *We the People* (Chicago: University of Chicago Press,

1958) proposes an alternative to the Beard thesis. Gordon S. Wood, *The Creation of the American Republic, 1776–1787* (Chapel Hill: University of North Carolina Press, 1969) moves even further away from Beard, and yet Wood also concludes that the general interpretation of Beard and the other "Progressive generation of historians—that the Constitution was in some sense an aristocratic document designed to curb the democratic excesses of the Revolution—still seems to me to be the most helpful framework for understanding the politics and ideology surrounding the Constitution."

That neither Wood nor anyone else will have the last word on the subject is reflected in the continuing debate over the "intent" of the Founders. William Crosskey and William Jeffrey, Jr., *Politics and the Constitution in the History of the United States,* 3 vols. (Chicago: University of Chicago Press, 1953–80), and William P. Murphy, *The Triumph of Nationalism* (Chicago: Quadrangle, 1967) contend that the Founders wanted to establish a vigorous, sovereign national government. Vincent Ostrom, *The Political Theory of a Compound Republic* (1971; rev. and enlarged ed., Lincoln: University of Nebraska Press, 1987), and Raoul Berger, *Federalism: The Founders' Design* (Norman: University of Oklahoma Press, 1987) argue that the Founders wanted to preserve the principle of federalism. Paul Eidelberg, *The Philosophy of the American Constitution* (New York: The Free Press, 1968) emphasizes the Founders' desire to create a "mixed regime" that balanced aristocratic and democratic impulses. Peter S. Onuf, *The Origins of the Federal Republic* (Philadelphia: University of Pennsylvania Press, 1983) adds his own twist, as have Jack P. Greene, *Peripheries and Center* (Athens: University of Georgia Press, 1986); John P. Diggins, *The Lost Soul of American Politics* (New York: Basic Books, 1984); and Richard Vetterli and Gary C. Bryner, *In Search of the Republic* (Totowa, N.J.: Rowman and Littlefield, 1987).

The battle over ratification has been treated in Robert Allen Rutland, *The Ordeal of the Constitution* (Norman: University of Oklahoma Press, 1966). The collection assembled in Jonathan Elliot, ed., *The Debates in the Several State Conventions on the Adoption of the Federal Constitution,* 2d ed., 5 vols. (Philadelphia: J. P. Lippincott, 1901) is being enlarged and improved by Merrill Jensen et al., eds., *Documentary History of the Ratification of the Constitution,* 15 vols. (Madison: State Historical Society of Wisconsin, 1976–). Bernard Schwartz, ed., *The Roots of the Bill of Rights,* 2 vols. (New York: Chelsea House, 1971) includes documents ranging from Magna Carta to state ratification of the first ten amendments. Robert Allen Rutland, *The Bill of Rights, 1776–1791* (Chapel Hill: University of North Carolina Press, 1955) and Irving Brant, *The Bill of Rights* (Indianapolis: Bobbs-Merrill Co., 1965) are both good.

Several anthologies of essays on the Constitution have been published for the Bicentennial: Richard Beeman, Stephen Botein, and Edward C. Carter II, eds., *Beyond Confederation* (Chapel Hill: University of North Carolina Press, 1987); Leonard Levy and Dennis J. Mahoney, eds., *The Framing and Ratification of the Constitution* (New York: Macmillan, 1987); and a revised edition of Levy, ed., *Essays on the Making of the Constitution* (New York: Oxford University Press, 1987). Michael Kammen, *A Machine That Would Go of Itself* (New York: Alfred A. Knopf, 1987) discusses how, over the years, the Constitution has become revered by the American public. Finally, for those dismayed by the length of even this short list there is Alfred H. Kelly, Winfred A. Harbison, and Herman Belz, *The American Constitution,* 6th ed. (New York: W. W. Norton, 1983), which presents a nice discussion of the making of the Constitution, put into a much larger context.

Index